Crisis and Transition

Polish Society in the 1980s

Crisis and Transition

Polish Society in the 1980s

Edited by
Jadwiga Koralewicz
Ireneusz Białecki
Margaret Watson

BERG

Oxford / New York / Hamburg

Distributed exclusively in the US and Canada by
St. Martin's Press New York

Published in 1987 by
Berg Publishers Limited
Market House, Deddington, Oxford OX5 4SW, UK
175 Fifth Avenue/Room 400, New York, NY 10010, USA
Schenefelder Landstr. 14K, 2000 Hamburg 55, FRG

British Library Cataloguing in Publication Data

Crisis and transition: Polish society in the 1980s–
  1. Poland — Social Conditions — 1980.
  I. Koralewicz, Jadwiga
  II. Białecki, Ireneusz   III. Watson, Margaret
  943.8'056   HN537.5

  ISBN 0–85496–525–4

Library of Congress Cataloging-in-Publication Data

Crisis and transition.

  Bibliography: p.
  Includes index.
  1. Poland—Social conditions—1980–
2. Poland—Politics and government—1980–
I. Koralewicz, Jadwiga.   II. Białecki, Ireneusz.
III. Watson, Margaret, 1948–
HN538.5.C75   1987   306'.09438   87–13843
ISBN 0–85496–525–4

Printed in Great Britain by Billings of Worcester

Contents

Foreword

As a sociologist I have had a number of opportunities to visit Poland. I was there in 1974 at a session of the Stratification Section of the International Sociological Association. I was there again with the ISA's Research Committee in the week during which the agreement with Solidarity was signed. And, finally, I made an extended visit to the Polish Academy during the period of martial law.

My own contacts were only part of a continuous process of contact between Polish sociology and the outside world. Polish sociology has a great and irrepressible history. It survived during the dark days of Stalinism even if under the guise of Dialectical and Historical Materialism. It continued during the 1960s and 1970s to pursue empirical research on what it claimed were Marxist themes. Many of its practitioners were very close to the Solidarity movement from its inception. And even under martial law a new generation of young sociologists were then to give a critical view of Polish social structure.

The present volume of essays is the brave product of this younger group of sociologists. It uses sociological theory and sociological techniques to deal with the problems which really face contemporary Poland. It deals with the structural nature of the present crisis; it discusses the problem of a regime working without legitimacy, yet desperately seeking to win consent; it discusses the history of workers management in Communist Poland and seeks to place Solidarity in relation to this tradition; and it faces up sharply to the problems faced by a command economy trying to find an alternative to market rationality. Running through all of the essays however is a concern which is expressed in Koralewicz's opening essay, namely the problem of how to live authentically in a society in which public behaviour is constrained by an alien and unwanted system. Her problem is a more general one than that which faces Poland or even

1

the Communist world.

Obviously these essays are of great importance for the sociology of contemporary Poland. One hopes that they will be widely read there not only by open critics of the regime but by those who have supported the regime. They deserve to be read by those whose goal is a Communist society both in order that they should re-evaluate the goal itself and that they should consider some of the unintended consequences of the means used for attaining the goal of Communism. But the book is important not for Poland only but for any sociologist who wishes to understand the options open to industrialising societies in the twentieth century.

I am very glad to have played a part in bringing this book to the attention of the English-speaking world. I am particularly grateful to Jadwiga Koralewicz for getting the material to me and to Peggy Watson for her work on the English version both in terms of language and the structure of the argument.

John Rex
University of Warwick

JADWIGA KORALEWICZ

Changes in Polish Social Consciousness during the 1970s and 1980s: Opportunism and Identity

It is possible to find many universal European cultural values in Poland's value system. There is little point in debating which of these is most important. Nevertheless, as a value, truth must be among the most highly esteemed. This is confirmed by the actions people take in defence of truth. The universality of this value lies in the fact that it touches every sphere of individual and collective life, it seems to transcend all other values. Without truth, personal values such as individual integrity, which demands a consistency between one's convictions, the expression of these convictions and one's actions, cannot be achieved. This consistency is in turn a necessary condition for a sense of individual identity when a person tries to answer the question: 'Who am I?'

In this chapter, I attempt to show what the chances are for individuals living in Poland in the 1970s and 1980s of finding an answer to this question concerning their identity.

Social Frustration in the 1970s

The high level of frustration in Polish society has been pointed out by S. Nowak (1979). More recent studies have shown that the level of frustration and anxiety and sense of danger was greater in the 1970s than it was during the 1960s. One indicator of the level of anxiety in a society is the suicide rate. A rise in this rate is usually caused by cultural changes and changes in the nature of social bonds and is always, as Rollo May has written, associated with traumatic psychological and emotional states. During the 1970s the suicide rate grew steadily in Poland, the first decline being recorded in 1980

3

(Jarosz 1981).[1]

The spread of rigorous and negative emotional attitudes towards offenders, a manifestation of displaced aggression, is another indicator of growing social frustration. In a study carried out in 1964 by the Centre for the Study of Public Opinion using a representative national sample, 16 per cent of respondents were in favour of the death penalty; by 1977 this had risen to 46 per cent (Podgórecki 1966: 79; Malec 1980: 61).

The opinions of young people are a particularly sensitive barometer of public attitudes. A comparison of the results of studies carried out by Świda in 1974 and 1978 show that a marked shift in the value systems and needs of young people took place during these four years. The comparison shows an increased need for security, a quiet existence and an escape from the realities of life. Young people were looking to their friends and to films and books for relaxation from the problems presented by everyday life; in the sphere of close personal contacts they looked for a lessening of feelings of anxiety and threat aroused by the outside world. These needs came to the fore in 1978 and were accompanied by a general lowering of aspirations. In this connection, Świda has stressed the fact that the anxiety expressed was not caused by technology or some other aspect of modern civilisation, but by problems of everyday life.[2]

The question arises as to the source of this increased frustration and feelings of threat and anxiety; an answer would be tantamount to an explanation of the causes of the crisis of 1980, which were in fact many. The present chapter is merely a small contribution to the social psychology of the Poles in the 1970s and 1980s. It is not concerned with the causes of the above-mentioned crisis, but rather it analyses the attitudes of those who were living in Poland during a period of rising psychological tension and endeavours to outline a more general framework of underlying factors. In this it relies on certain theories of cognitive psychology.

The 1970s cannot be viewed as a particularly repressive period in Poland. In comparison with Stalinist times — if we restrict ourselves to postwar history — this was a period of relative liberalisation of the system, of greater openness to the outside world and

---

1. Jarosz calculated on the basis of Central Statistical Agency data that the first decline in the Polish suicide rate for thirty years occurred in 1980.
2. The studies were conducted in Warsaw secondary schools in 1974, and in similar schools in different Polish towns in 1978 (see Świda 1987).

increased contacts with the West. There was no intensification of terror, police invigilation, social conflict, or manifestation of hatred. And yet the institutional system functioned so that people faced external coercion on an increasing scale. This was due to 'pressure based on violence of some other kind', as Ossowski (1967a: 150–1) has defined it in his distinction between coercion based on direct physical violence and that which is not. That is to say, the state monopoly of the basic institutions of public life deprived the individual of the opportunity of changing a situation which he or she did not accept and of substituting another. The lack of such organisations as free trade unions and the frequent violations of the rule of law meant that people saw their situation very clearly as being one from which there was no way out, and where there was no way of defending themselves against possible threats. This sense of being locked in was aggravated by an inability to control events at grass-roots level, a lack of self-management and the blocking of spontaneous activity both within and outside the enterprise.[3] It must be borne in mind here that regardless of the form of pressure used, external coercion places the individual in a situation in which he or she is obliged to act in a way which is at variance with his or her opinion (Ossowski 1967a: 150–1). Actions which conflict with one's opinion give rise to a form of cognitive dissonance. As Malewski has written:

> one of the applications of the concept of cognitive dissonance is in situations where people act in a way which is not in accord with their opinions, regardless of whether they do this out of fear or in order to obtain particular advantages. The relationship of 'outwardly we approve of a certain programme' to 'inwardly we condemn this programme' is one of cognitive dissonance. (Malewski 1975: 212)

The question arises as to what form of cognitive dissonance was most typical of the Poles during the 1970s. I do not think that any new form emerged during this time. However, it does seem that

---

3. For a discussion of the changes in institutional and organisational structures and the power system as the main sources of coercion, see Pańków (1982a). It seems that the period under consideration was marked by the increased significance of controlled processes in institutional and organisational structures for the processes taking place in the class and stratum structures of society. The spontaneous re-structuration which was observable in the late 1950s and the 1960s was of a limited nature. Since people at the two levels of social structure were unable to meet their basic needs, small groups played the main supporting and compensatory role for individuals.

existing cracks and discrepancies were aggravated, resulting in a higher level of frustration and anxiety.[4]

The figure opposite refers to certain observable trends of the 1970s:

(1) The normatively defined social structure — that is, the desired representation of the facts — was at variance with the perceived representation of the facts (Koralewicz-Zębik 1984).

(2) The perception of the social structure was consistent with social facts and changes which were then taking place.[5]

(3) The normative structure as it functioned in social consciousness was based on the norms and principles of socialist ideology (Koralewicz-Zębik 1984).

(4) Official propaganda channels (mainly the mass media), some publications (including academic publications) and data issued by the Central Statistical Agency among others, acted together to create an image of reality which was at odds with the facts. This was achieved through data fabrication and censorship which involved the suppression of certain data and analyses.[6]

(5) The image of reality projected through the channels of propaganda accorded with socialist ideology.[7]

---

4. Anxiety is a state of mental discomfort which results from a long period of frustration or tension which decreases the sense of one's own value. An individual often does not realise his or her anxiety, which may manifest itself in many undesirable responses. This is what is known as latent anxiety. Open anxiety comes close to fear, but apart from its durability, differs from the latter in that the responses which it evokes are not related to any definite danger (see Jedlicki 1961; Kępiński 1977; Stein et al. (eds) 1965).

5. The dynamics of differences of income and the perception of income difference may serve as an example. The early 1970s saw an increase in income differentials in different social categories. Inter-group differences fell after 1975 but small groups of privileged people had incomes far above the average. In this connection see Czołoszyński (n.d.); Góralska (1981). Hence, while some groups might have felt relatively better off and some worse off in the early 1970s, by the late 1970s nearly everyone except the most privileged felt worse off. Results of studies on social consciousness have shown that in the 1970s people felt economic differences to be increasing. This led to the formation of a bi-polar structure comprising the privileged and the rest of the nation. See the mimeographed communiqué of the Centre for the Study of Public Opinion concerning social inequalities and injustice in the consciousness of the Polish people issued in Warsaw in 1980.

6. Data substantiating this claim and revealed after August 1980 are too numerous to mention. See the report on social communication in Poland prepared by the Association of Polish Journalists, Part II, Section 6; see also J. Surdykowski's report in *Kontrasty*, 1981, no. 8, and the series of articles under the joint title 'Co Kto Wiedział' (Who Knew What) in *Przegląd Techniczny*, 1981.

7. This claim has been documented by Strzelecki (fortcoming).

The social structure: discrepancies between ideology, social facts and social perception

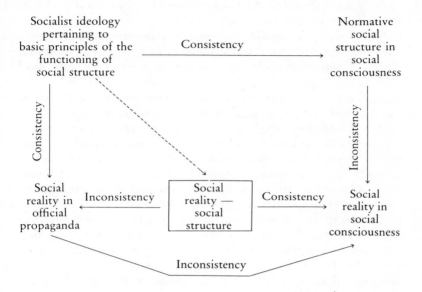

(6) The population was continuously subjected to this propaganda.

The essential feature of Polish social consciousness in the 1970s lay in the fact that the dividing line between (a) the facts and the distorted representation of the facts, and (b) what existed and what should have existed, was not obliterated. Hence the operations intended to manipulate the consciousness of the masses had proved ineffective on a national scale. These two forms of cognitive dissonance persisted in social consciousness, giving rise to extreme tension. This also served to motivate action. Discrepancies between incoming information and pre-existing information in people's 'cognitive network', — that is, information treated as true and as such giving rise to certain expectations *vis-à-vis* incoming information, are the source of *cognitive motivation*. Discrepancies between what is observed and what is desired are the source of *practical motivation*. Cognitive motivation leads the individual to seek information and intensifies his or her interest in the actual state of affairs. Practical motivation leads to action aimed at changing the existing

7

state of affairs and its subordination to the norms and ideals espoused by the individual (Reykowski 1978: 238). A certain level of discrepancy is therefore desirable since it serves to motivate action and this in turn may bring gratification.

Any change in the existing institutional system, in the most general sense of the term, had small chance of success in the 1970s. Practical motivation was thus blocked, and extreme frustration ensued, becoming a powerful motor of action in 1980. This was not the case as far as cognitive motivation was concerned; here, discrepancies stimulated people to seek information. Knowledge was acquired through individual observation and experience; information was channelled through a vast informal network consisting of small groups of family, friends or workmates, the Church, the Western mass media and publications outside the reach of state censorship. The 1970s were marked in Poland by a seeking of information emanating from unofficial sources.

The emergence of new information sources and new means of opinion moulding in the 1970s gave extra impetus to this cognitive motivation. It appears that the continuing discrepancies arising from the co-existence of two information systems in people's 'cognitive network' was not in itself a source of extreme tension, although these discrepancies grew following changes in the way official information was handled, particularly in the wake of the events of 1976. I am thinking here of the intensification of what is referred to as the propaganda of success. Perhaps for some the stress was destructive; that is to say, it overcame their psychological resistance and led to negative responses. But it seems more likely that cognitive dissonance was eliminated by an evaluation of the truthfulness of each of the two information systems. That which emanated from official propaganda sources was treated as untrue, and this sufficed for the elimination of the negative tension resulting from cognitive dissonance.[8]

8. This general statement is at variance with what might be termed 'consistency theories' such as Festinger's theory of cognitive dissonance and Heider's theory of cognitive equilibrium. These theories assume that all discrepancies are sources of negative tension, and the desire to rid oneself of this tension results in the formation of mechanisms of self-deception. The theory of cognitive activeness embodies an opposing idea. Without going into detail, I should point out that further analyses of the social facts in Poland seem to indicate that these theories are complementary and each has its application. In the opinion of Reykowski, it is only when the discrepancy between one's expectations and incoming information on the one hand, and what is observable on the other, reaches a certain point that negative tension arises, which in turn may lead to decreased activeness and a sense of hopelessness.

Nevertheless, tension persisted, and there were at least three reasons for this. In the first place, the continuous reception of false information is offensive to a person's dignity, since it indicates that the sender does not take his or her cognitive abilities seriously. In the second place, channels of feedback information were blocked — the Association of Polish Journalists' report on social communication indicated the mechanisms for the creation of a one-way information system from the top downwards.[9] Since this was the case, tensions were dissipated in small groups; opinions which could not be expressed in public were voiced in private conversations. Thirdly, tension was growing because people were obliged to act on the basis of this false information. This institutionally generated 'substitute reality' which was based on fiction and dysfunction, called for actions which caused individuals inner conflict: they felt their actions to be senseless, their sense of frustration rose and their self-esteem was diminished. There was also a detrimental effect on people's sense of dignity. In essence, cognitive dissonance gives rise to an impaired sense of personal dignity. In the 1970s almost everyone in Poland experienced such a threat to their dignity. This explains the intensity of the need for affiliation, a normal reaction to a threat to the ego.[10]

A Tentative Typology of Responses to External Coercion

How did the Poles respond to external coercion? Below I present one of several possible typologies of attitudes expressed by those playing formal roles in institutions and organisations. This typology supposes that the institutional system has produced a generalised situation of external coercion as its frame of reference.

A person in a situation of external coercion may act in one of several ways. Firstly, he or she may try to change the institutional system. In Poland such attitudes have, as a rule, ended in utter defeat. The system whereby directives are transmitted from the monopolistic central authorities downwards, precludes the possibility of social actions intended to change that system. If a person cannot accommodate himself or herself, having failed to change the existing situation, he or she may choose the following option.

9. See the report on social communication in Poland referred to on p. 6, n. 6.
10. Affiliation needs occupied a prime position in the need system of Polish people. In this connection see S. Nowak (1979) and Koralewicz-Zębik (1979).

Secondly, he or she may withdraw from the system, abandoning actions intended to change it, or continuing such actions outside the system, as for example in the case of the so-called democratic opposition. The decision to withdraw from the official system has not been an easy one to take. Apart from private enterprise and the Church, all other institutions are controlled by the state and the party power apparatus. People today must live within a system of institutions. Opting out of one institution entails acting within another. This kind of change did not affect a person's mental state since the principles according to which all institutions function and the problems involved, are the same. However, one could move out of the system and become active, for example, in the private sector of the economy as an employee or entrepreneur. Such decisions were in fact made. The 1970s saw an increase in the number of graduates starting up craft workshops and farms. Other people took odd jobs such as milk rounds or seasonal work. This gave them independence and was usually associated with a change in life-style. Finally, one could go abroad, for a few years or for good. Although this was usually done to earn money, at a deeper motivational level such decisions represented an escape from a native country where people were dissatisfied and had often tried to change some elements of the system. In this way many well-qualified professionals have left Poland. This is a separate question which has been little studied despite the long-standing Polish tradition in the study of emigrants.

The third option was resorted to by people who were aware that total change was impossible and that certain principles had to be more or less accepted even if they were not endorsed. Such people did not withdraw from the system but tried to modify it in a small way. In order to avoid defeat, they acted in two ways: (a) they evaded or reinterpreted various regulations whose proliferation was paralysing social and economic life, and (b) they availed themselves of their own informal personal contacts. In addition to coteries of persons using their official status to avail themselves of illegal advantages and gain, and coteries of those subservient to the system, which we discuss below, there were also informal networks of so-called honest people. This term is used with reference to those who tried to retain independence of opinion and action and who could afford to be courageous and persistent. Their attitude might be termed one of 'controlled courage'.

Each of these three kinds of response might be termed 'active goal-orientated behaviour'.[11] Here an obstacle is viewed as something to be removed. People who act in this way do not respond with anxiety in situations they find difficult. If they fear something, they are able to identify what it is they fear. In their actions they take a calculated risk that they will be punished for what they do. Many factors contribute to such attitudes: a greater resistance to stress, a stronger internalisation of certain norms, fewer accumulated threats, a greater opportunity for compensatory action.

There are no empirical data which would allow us to link particular attitudes with socioeconomic position. The 'democratic opposition' included manual workers and intellectuals alike. Among those going abroad were both qualified engineers and manual workers. The third group of what might be called 'reformers' might include a teacher who, in defiance of official instructions and textbooks, tries to convey true information concerning historical events, or it might include a workman in a theatre who, in order to get the set ready on time, asks a former workmate to supply him with nails — even nails being in short supply.

But the response to external coercion may also take the form of conformism. Fromm and Reisman, among others, have pointed to the fact that the degree of conformism exhibited by an individual in a given situation is closely related to the level of anxiety experienced in that situation. Numerous empirical studies have confirmed that conformism is positively correlated with a lack of security, anxiety and low self-esteem (Vaughan and White 1966). Conformism is a defensive response to anxiety on the part of the ego, as two American researchers have put it (Smith and Richards 1967).

Conformist behaviour can be evoked either by manipulating rewards and punishments or by manipulating anxiety. On a large scale the manipulation of anxiety is by far the more effective in ensuring compliance. Here obedience is seemingly spontaneous, dispensing with the need for threat or the lure of reward. Such responses are termed 'threat-orientated', not 'goal-orientated'; they function as a defence mechanism which reduces anxiety.

Those who adopt the conformist attitude may be classified as follows:

(1) They may be those who realise that they are acting in a way

11. Newcomb (1956: 350–9) makes a distinction between orientations towards a goal and towards danger.

which conflicts with their convictions. Such people will be termed 'opportunists' here. They act in accordance with external demands, but they also have a private sphere where no mask is required, where behaviour ceases to be instrumental and where they may reflect on their own behaviour or that of others, or indeed, on the situation in general.

(2) They may be those who have changed their opinions and who therefore feel that in their actions they have adopted the right goals and methods. These are conformists in the strict sense of the term. Here instrumentalism becomes the supreme directive for action, and there is a consequent total conformism, total adjustment and the loss of a sense of dual morality. This change of conviction accounts for the fact that lies and fiction are treated as if they were the truth.

The changes of conviction and resulting conformist behaviour which anxiety brings about may cover a large area of the personality. This leads to a kind of psychic impotence where people believe any statement about the real world which has been transmitted to them, adopt the goals and values inculcated in them, accept modes of action put forward by the person or institution which manipulates them, experience the emotional states which have been preordained for them and identify with designated persons and groups.

The fundamental difference between these two attitudes lies in the degree of change which takes place in the cognitive structures of the individual concerning the ways in which the real world and accepted goals and modes of action are interpreted. Conformists in the strict sense of the word reconstruct their consciousness, as it were, at least with regard to a threatening situation. The transition from opportunism to conformity is a fluid one and as Malewski (1975) has written, 'the very undertaking of actions which are at variance with one's convictions increases the probability of a change in those convictions'.

Succumbing to the exigencies of an external situation is a defensive response and reduces anxiety, but the consciousness of having thus succumbed to pressure and having acted at variance with one's own convictions itself causes new tension which has to be reduced. New defence mechanisms become necessary.

The defence mechanisms which were most common among the opportunists of the 1970s were rationalisation, projection and repression. We can distinguish six main ways in which these mechanisms manifested themselves:

(1) The maximisation of rewards. Those who rationalised in this way were probably those who were orientated towards improving their position and obtaining better jobs and more privileges; that is to say, they were more achievement-orientated.

(2) The maximisation of punishment. This tended to refer to those who had already achieved something in life. For them the loss of privilege and status meant a lowering of social worth. It might also refer to those whose present position was vulnerable due to their having inadequate professional qualifications, or because of competition. Persons more susceptible to stress and with a greater sense of vulnerability might also be included in this category.

(3) Frequent reference to the fact that everyone acts in the same way; that is, everyone gives in to external pressure.

(4) Frequent reference to higher motives; explaining one's actions in terms of being a means of achieving a laudable goal such as the good of the family, the good of one's children, the good of socialist society, the vanquishing of an enemy and so on. A particular version of this form of rationalisation was to change the declared goal of one's actions. The impossibility of meeting such needs as that for rational action, creative work or independent decision-making caused a reorientation of goals: unacceptable tasks were performed in exchange for peace and quiet, free time, trips abroad or large sums of money. This therefore was a kind of reckoning of profits and losses. This reckoning could be taken to the point where a situation hitherto viewed as inconvenient came to be desirable; the minimum of activity which initially would go against one's convictions, might turn into uncommonly operative and effective behaviour.

(5) The manifestation of a feeling of helplessness and a belief that external reality cannot be changed. The person believes that the system is so powerful that any resistance is senseless and the only sensible thing to do, the only way to survive, is to give in. This attitude tended to be accompanied by passivity, a lowering of activity in relation to one's potential and the seeking of a place in which to survive. This feeling of helplessness led to passive resistance.

13

(6) The tendency to belittle the importance of behaviour at odds with one's convictions, either because of its significance in the situation taken as a whole, or from the point of view of the individual's value system.

The scale of opportunism may include widely divergent forms of behaviour, from the person who feels that he or she is acting under duress and tries to restrict these acts to a minimum, to the person who evinces a thorough-going demoralisation, cynicism, and consciously exploits this coercive situation in order to derive the greatest possible advantage for himself or herself.

Different institutions and specific social roles were marked by different degrees of coercion. Small groups also played some part in shaping opportunistic attitudes. People would justify themselves to their families, their friends and acquaintances, and would look for arguments in favour of their opportunistic behaviour. This process of mental purification reduced a person's sense of danger since he or she was among people who were in a similarly difficult situation. But it also consolidated opportunistic attitudes by reinforcing the conviction that no other reaction was possible.

This typology of attitudes towards external coercion, like any typology, says nothing about the distribution of such attitudes in society. Nor does it tell us whether they may co-exist within one personality, or how they may change according to social circumstances. If people could be classified by type according to which attitude prevails, then we might be able to speak of opportunists, conformists, independent-minded oppositionists and so on. However, it is more often the case that the same person may adopt different attitudes at different times.

Marked fluidity of attitude might denote controlled courage or opportunism. The lack of empirical data makes it impossible to advance any correct diagnosis. Although controlled courage was a common attitude during the 1970s, opportunism it would seem was even more prevalent. Both attitudes were accompanied by a dissonant consciousness typical of the period: an awareness of the dissonance between reality and fiction, between the realm of action and the realm of ideology. The continuing awareness of the lack of agreement between these spheres of experience gives rise to severe tension, the cause of which need not be fully realised.

This dissonant consciousness coupled with opportunistic reactions to external institutional coercion seems to have been the *signum temporis* of the 1970s. It is probably legitimate to talk of a flowering of an opportunistic ethos marking both attitudes and behaviour. The most important consequence of this ethos in terms of individual psychology was an internal split of the personality and a loss of identity. Living in the public and private world alternately, in the real world and the official world, the world of people and of institutions, and acting against one's convictions, the individual was constantly donning and doffing a mask; he or she had continually to deal with the pervading dualism of evaluations and attitudes, with double-talk and so on (Wnuk-Lipiński 1982).

During the 1970s people became much less sensitive to their own opinions and those of others. They attached little importance to those distinctive, individual characteristics of each person.[12] Differences between people did not so much involve differences of view but rather the extent to which opinions might be revealed according to social role. For example, the director of an enterprise found himself in more roles where he was obliged to adopt officially approved attitudes than did an ordinary worker. However, everyone was linked by a shared dissatisfaction and sense of helplessness.

External Coercion under Martial Law

Martial law was imposed in Poland on 13 December 1981. This meant an intensification of external coercion. The Poles were subjected to a pressure which Ossowski (1967a: 150) would have defined as being based on direct physical violence, using such penal sanctions as death, corporal punishment and imprisonment. This pressure was designed to serve several purposes:

(1) The isolation, mainly through internment, of several thousand Solidarity leaders from the several-million-strong membership and the subjection of tens of thousands of movement activists to strict supervision.

(2) Physical coercion helped to end resistance and to break up sit-ins of the workforces of many enterprises who were protesting against the delegalisation of Solidarity, the intern-

---

12. For example, studies carried out in 1974 showed that political opinions were viewed as being of no importance in the system of social differentiation (see Otawska 1976). In the early 1960s differences of opinion were still clearly noticed (see S. Nowak 1965).

ment of its leaders and the suspension of all independent social organisations representing the interests of various social groups.

(3) The threat or actual use of physical coercion made it possible to paralyse communication. This was done by disconnecting telephones, banning any permanent move to another town, imposing curfews, carrying out personal searches in the streets and at home, closing virtually all the editorial offices of daily newspapers, magazines and publishing houses.

(4) Food prices were drastically raised in the second month of martial law. The threat of recourse to physical coercion prevented a repetition of the social protests which had occurred in 1976 and 1980 in response to such rises.

(5) Physical coercion in the shape of internment, interrogation, searches and trials eliminated all forms of symbolic support for the ideas of Solidarity.[13]

In addition to physical coercion, the authorities also applied economic coercion. This involved either the dismissal from employment of Solidarity activists, or the imposition of compulsory work through, for example, the militarisation of certain enterprises and institutions. The price rises, which pauperised the overwhelming majority of society and large families and old-age pensioners in particular, themselves constituted a form of economic pressure.

During the first few months of martial law this wholesale use of actual or potential physical violence, the suspension of many basic civil rights and the use of economic coercion intimidated virtually the whole of Polish society. This fear and existential danger was associated with the blocking of all those needs and values which had started to be met on such a vast scale in 1980–1 for the first time since the People's Republic had come into being. For martial law had resulted in the suspension or dissolution of all those organisations which had come into being in 1980–1 in order to express and defend the different interests of various groups in Polish society. This physical restraint was therefore associated with the extreme frustration which was caused by this situation of severe relative deprivation. As many studies have shown, the withdrawal of certain privileges arouses greater stress and is the source of more dangerous

---

13. The goals and functions of severe coercion under martial law are given after Pańków (1983).

frustration than deprivation which is not preceded by the experience of having a specific need satisfied.

During the later months of martial law and after its repeal, the government also attempted to resolve social conflict without the use of force. There was an attempt to create a so-called national consensus. This purpose was served by the apparent tendency to assimilate the ideals of Solidarity. However, this was not real change and did not alter the essential nature of the social system or the monopolistic position of the central state institutions. The authorities put great organisational and propaganda effort into trying to achieve these appearances. The methods they used included a system of so-called social consultation, new social organisations, new trade unions, employee self-management and a whole series of new laws. In this way the government reinstated the institutional coercion of the 1970s.

Attitudes towards External Coercion in 1983–4

After the experiences of 1980–1 and martial law, Polish society was no longer the society it had been in the 1970s. Social consciousness had undergone profound changes. More than ever before, people's consciousness influenced their behaviour and also determined the structural transformation of society. Changes in consciousness with regard to the perception of values and attitudes seem to be a relatively permanent effect of the Polish revolution and counter-revolution of the early 1980s.

In attempting to present the main trends in these changes, I shall refer to studies for the most part carried out in 1983 and 1984, after the repeal of martial law when the situation had been 'normalised', that is when state-institutional coercion had once more taken the place of physical and economic coercion.

Under martial law, which had been preceded by a period of intense democratic social learning, the process had taken place of which Ossowski wrote: 'on the level of society conditions of extreme external coercion usually cause a polarisation of mental types' (1967a: 156). This polarisation of attitudes persists to the present day. It is true that the typology of attitudes to external coercion presented above in relation to conditions prevailing in the 1970s reflects all the differences which can be found in 1982–4. However, the dominant attitudes are not the same as before.

17

The number of people who are now trying to avoid the over-whelming influence of institutional coercion has increased; they want to achieve independence from the state in their basic life roles. Such persons differ from each other in the degree, or rather proportion, to which their behaviour is pro-social or egocentric, but they are united by a common set of values and the wish to become independent, or reduce the influence of the institutional power of the state on their everyday lives.

Some of these people actively continue to put into effect the ideas of Solidarity within the framework of so-called illegal structures. Many of them have lost their jobs, or are on an old-age or disability pension; they take odd jobs and live on very modest means, concentrating their activities on various kinds of socio-political and charity work, and clandestine publishing. These activities do not bring instantaneously visible effects in the form of institutional changes in the social system — this would be impossible without strong external coercion. Their actions are, rather, intended to educate society, to provide people with information which cannot be found in the official mass media and continually to reaffirm in social consciousness the values which Solidarity was fighting for.

Those who have taken jobs in the non-socialised sector of the economy and in firms run by Poles from abroad are also seeking greater independence from state institutions. The number of people who are self-employed is also steadily rising, particularly among graduates. In addition to financial motivation, they are acting in accordance with many values which were revived during 1980–1; these include initiative, creativity, meaningful action, the possibility of influencing the course and effects of one's work, personal responsibility and a greater correlation between material benefits and work input.

A third way of freeing oneself from the influence of institutional structures is to leave the country, either for an extended period or for good. A study conducted among Warsaw University students in 1983 showed that 32.4 per cent of them wanted to leave the country for an extended period, while in another study carried out in the Opole voivodeship, 33 per cent of young workers expressed the same wish (Lindenberg 1986; Michałczyk 1983).

On the other hand, the category of persons to which we have referred as conformists *sensu stricto* also seems to have been grow-ing. These people act in the belief that the goals and methods which have been imposed on them are right. They are convinced that they are acting in accordance with their own convictions. In joining the new trade unions or the Patriotic Movement for National Renewal (PRON),[14] they believe in the possibility of self-management, social consensus and the good will of the authorities. These people accept most of the government's actions and are convinced of their legitimacy.

The fact that the scale of opportunism and hence the number of persons we may term opportunists has become much reduced is of particular importance. It should be remembered that the overwhelming majority of Poles remain closely dependent on the state institutional system. It has been Solidarity's bequest that after its delegalisation there persist personal ties between people who are linked by their shared experience — first the creation of Solidarity groups and work within these groups, then the experiences of martial law, the protests, the dismissals and the discrimination at work. These personal links form the nuclei of new opinion-forming reference groups. People who do not manifest out-and-out conformism *vis-à-vis* the authorities try to win the approval of these groups, which in this way inhibit full-scale opportunism. As a result of the forms of rationalisation mentioned above which justify opportunistic reactions to external coercion, most people exaggerate the possible penalties for disobedience or manifest attitudes of helplessness and passivity as they seek a place where they can survive.

The attitude which we have termed 'controlled courage' seems to be as common now as it was before. However, the motivation of those who do not easily give in to external coercion has changed. Attempts to partially alter the situation in which one plays one's role are not so much undertaken for the good of the institution, for these are identified even more closely than before with the power apparatus, but rather because of the need to maintain such personal values as dignity, independence, truth and justice. Some of these people are deeply sympathetic to the ideas of Solidarity. They read the underground press and participate in various ways in Solidarity's underground structures.

---

14. PRON — Patriotyczny Ruch Odrodzenia Narodowego (Patriotic Movement for National Renewal), a pro-government political grouping formed during martial law as a successor to the Front Jedności Narodowej (Front of National Unity) [Ed. (M.W.)].

The Polarisation of Attitudes under Strong Coercion

One might ask what were the mechanisms behind the polarisation of attitudes which took place between 1982 and 1984. In accordance with what has been said at the outset, I shall seek an interpretation of these psycho-social phenomena in theories of cognition. Such theories assume that people's attitudes and values are determined by the way they organise their knowledge and information. Now, both the experiences which people had during the Solidarity period and during the first few months of martial law brought changes to their cognitive system, each in their own way. These changes acted in the same direction and their cumulative effect was to raise the level of the *organisation of cognitive structures* among Polish people. This meant a greater ability to think about social matters using abstract concepts, being able to discover the rules and general mechanisms governing social life. It meant seeing social reality in all its complexity, perceiving the mutual interdependence of different aspects of life and the interconnectedness of different social groups. It also meant being able to see one's own situation in its social context.

Apart from the new credible information sources, there were two factors in the Solidarity period which were particularly important in giving people a new cognitive perspective. One was the fact that inter-group or inter-class integration and increased social communication led to a better acquaintance with the ways of thinking and behaving of members of those social categories with which people had previously had no contact. For in the 1970s communication had been concentrated within small groups. Secondly, a very large number of people appeared in new social roles — as citizens conscious of their rights, as active members of social and political organisations, as employees responsible for their workplaces, as genuinely active voluntary workers and so on. As we know, the adoption of new social roles broadens the individual's cognitive perspective (see Turner 1962).

A permanent change in the way in which social phenomena were perceived was also brought about by the threatening nature of the situation in which virtually all social categories, but particularly the striking workers, mothers worried about feeding their children, the old and the sick, found themselves. Under martial law the whole of society, and former Solidarity activists in particular, felt threatened. Empirical studies of the social consequences of threatening situations have shown that when such a situation comes to an end the community which has experienced it is no longer the same. Moral integration and anomie is followed by reflection. There emerges a diversification of opinions and attitudes concerning what has been experienced. But regardless of this, everyone shares a genuine intellectual stimulation, an increased ability to analyse social facts and less inclination to condemn others and pass oversimplified judgements (Kiciński 1987).

It is often held in the literature that an increased ability to analyse social facts, a widening of cognitive horizons, being able to see what was previously invisible and having a more realistic idea of the nature of social facts usually gives people greater control over social reality. Greater knowledge of social life, it is argued, reduces our fear of it. What is known can be better controlled and is felt to be less threatening. The unknown is one of the basic sources of anxiety (Kępiński 1977: 217). And yet the knowledge which the Poles had in 1984 concerning social life and the mechanisms which govern it, raises rather than lowers their anxiety level. This is because theirs is a tragic knowledge. What it shows so glaringly is an unaccepted social order and a stable political system which is not undergoing any permanent change.

The most recent studies suggest that between 1978 and 1984 there was a marked deterioration in the mood of the Polish people. There was a particular increase in feelings of helplessness and depression. While in the 1978 study 16.5 per cent of respondents felt a sense of helplessness always or very often, the corresponding figure for 1984 was 27.8 per cent. On the other hand, while in 1978, 47 per cent of respondents never or very rarely felt helpless, the corresponding figure for 1984 dropped to 30.3 per cent.[15] Other replicated studies showed that in 1975 one in every ten manual workers and members of the intelligentsia was dissatisfied with his or her life, while in 1982 this was true of one in four respondents.[16]

Given this situation, who are the people who are more prone to increased levels of anxiety, and who is less likely to suffer psychologically? A study was carried out using a representative national sample in which respondents were asked to assess how decisive various factors were for personal success in Poland. The results

15. These data pertain to representative samples of males gainfully employed outside agriculture (Koralewicz-Zębik 1983a).
16. The study was based on national samples of households and was carried out in 1982 (see Sikorska 1983).

21

showed that in popular consciousness there are now two opposing conceptions concerning the reasons for personal success in present-day Poland. One of these conceptions points to the illegitimate factors governing success; the other points to factors which enjoy social approval and in the accepted system of values. The latter include firmness of purpose, innate ability, reliability and diligence, boldness of decision and independence of thought, and the courage to speak the truth. The former includes inherited status, cunning, an instrumental approach to the making of friends and the expression of views which are currently approved of. These two sets of characteristics are put forward by people who differ primarily in the degree to which they experience frustration, anxiety, a sense of helplessness and a sense of threat. Those who see the functioning of unacceptable criteria for the distribution of rewards show a higher level of anxiety. And conversely, those for whom perceived reality is in accordance with socially approved norms are less anxious.

Similar relationships obtained when responses concerning the social order were analysed. A sense of helplessness is most strongly associated with the belief that there is a lack of freedom of speech and association in Poland, but also with the belief that there is no equality before the law, that the government does not act in the interests of the majority and that earnings are not dependent on education, qualifications and work input.[17]

This brings us to the next question. Why is it that Polish society is seen by some in terms of an accepted order, the rule of law, just rewards for work done, freedom of association and a government which acts in the interests of the majority, while in the eyes of others the same society has no rule of law, is full of injustice and has a government which is not accepted by the people and which does not allow the formation of organisations which might represent the interests of various social groups?[18]

The results of the study show that adherence to one or other of these two images of the social order is not greatly influenced by a person's position within the system of stratification. However,

17. The study was based on a representative sample of households and was carried out early in 1984 by E. Skotnicka-Illasiewicz, J. Koralewicz, K. Janicka, B. Mach and E. Wnuk-Lipiński at the Polish Academy of Sciences Institute of Philosophy and Sociology, and had the title, 'Social Inequalities, a Sense of Ties and Self- confidence' (original in Polish); see report (Wnuk-Lipiński (ed.) 1987).
18. Perception of the social order depends on many structural and psychological factors. At this point my purpose is to mention an additional possible interpretation which is currently applicable to a particularly large section of society.

there is a relationship between attitudes to external coercion, one's vision of social reality and level of anxiety.

The perception of a non-legitimated social order is not a comfortable one; it gives rise to tension and frustration. A picture of an accepted order eliminates discrepancies between one's values and the social reality one perceives.[19] However, in order to achieve this harmonious state, one has to reform one's cognitive structure (network). When the various dimensions of social reality are consistent, inner calm is restored and anxiety reduced. Physical coercion under martial law, and the reactions of fear and anxiety which it caused, resulted in the people who were less resistant to these influences reconstructing the cognitive layer of their consciousness. This allowed them to accept what the government had done. They succumbed to official propaganda and treated a whole series of bogus government actions designed to create a so-called national consensus, with utmost seriousness and good faith. It is among such people that we find conformists who succumb to external coercion. As we know, conformity reduces anxiety. It should now be clear why there is a lower level of anxiety among people who perceive the prevailing social order as legitimate.

However, for the overwhelming majority of people the broadening of cognitive horizons was a source of psychological strength; it helped them to overcome their fears and to withstand psychological manipulation. The fact that they knew more about the way the socio-political system functioned led them to reject official propaganda by boycotting the press and television, or to devalue the information they broadcast. In this way the cognitive dissonance which might have arisen from the necessary co-existence of two information systems was greatly reduced. However, dissonance between accepted norms and perceived reality persists. It is all the more acute in that values which had been hitherto accepted have been more firmly internalised and a better knowledge of the facts has led them to perceive the functioning of unacceptable social mechanisms.[20] This dissonance gives rise to acute psychological

19. This interpretation assumed a social consensus with regard to the values espoused by various social groups. It seems that there is an area of fundamental values which are shared in Polish society.
20. Studies carried out in 1978 and 1983 among university students showed that a change of opinion concerning socialism generally and its Polish version is linked to a change of perception of the Polish socio-political system. In the 1970s the students ascribed the difficulties in which the country found itself to the citizens and to the system in almost equal measure, tending rather to emphasise the fault of citizens.

discomfort. Taken in conjunction with the frustration bred of the conviction that open rebellion is impossible, this explains why some people want to leave the country and others engage in a long-term struggle; why some concentrate on survival and a minimisation of effort expended on behalf of the state institutions where they work, while others as far as their situation will allow, fight on within the framework of these institutions for basic values and civil rights.

Consistency of Attitude and Variation of Political Opinions in 1983–4: Opportunism and Identity

The opportunistic ethos, which was based on a split in the integrity of the personality and which introduced ambiguity into human attitudes, was limited during this period. Sensitivity to the discrepancies between words and deeds could be observed much more frequently. Many more people than before disapproved of these discrepancies. There did, however, exist both an expectation and a need on the part of people to be able to define themselves in various social roles and situations. Attitudes were much more consistent. Individuals showed themselves more willing to defend their own opinions even if it involved the risk of unpleasantness or reprisals of some kind.[21]

For the first time in twenty years public-opinion research showed that political opinion was a factor which divided Polish society. This dimension of social inequality began to be perceived more frequently than education or power, which apart from income, were the dominant dimensions of inequality in the 1970s. Only social divisions which are based on financial criteria have precedence over political attitudes and views.[22]

This picture of social reality is confirmed in other research which was carried out at the same time and which involved manual workers and qualified engineers in five large industrial enterprises in Poland. In this study 49 per cent of respondents stated that during

---

Today the political and economic system is clearly perceived as the cause of the difficulties (Lindenberg 1986).

21. Studies of university students showed that in 1978, 27.8 per cent of respondents who were ready to undertake public action thought that they should do this regardless of personal risk and the reaction of the authorities. In 1983, 82 per cent shared this opinion, although fewer students were ready to undertake public action (see Lindenberg 1986).

22. Results of the study referred to on p. 22, n. 17.

the previous three years their assessment and interpretation of events had caused misunderstanding and conflict between themselves and their friends and acquaintances. Thus differences of view and attitude undermined the ties of ·small groups which seem so durable in Poland. This fact testifies to the strength of people's commitment to their own opinions.[23]

The main criterion for the variation of political views lay in a person's attitude to the authorities and the legitimacy or credibility of those currently in power. Attitudes to the authorities were manifested in reactions to the imposition of martial law and the measures which were designed to get the country out of its state of crisis. Reactions to the latter determined a person's degree of optimism and level of activity and cooperation with the institutional system.

It is hard to find those factors which point with any degree of precision to those social groups which are particularly liable to accept the government's programme, and the measures which are intended to generate the greatest number of supporters for this programme. They include persons holding higher-rank managerial positions, members of the Polish United Workers' Party and the new trade unions which replaced Solidarity, and the new social organisations. They also include women rather than men and the elderly rather than the young. The degree of genuine commitment to the social movement in 1980–1 is another criterion. Those who were more involved at that time are probably less likely to accept the present social order. The same applies to young people in view of the continuing economic crisis and the lack of opportunity for rapid self-betterment; particularly with regard to income. Manual workers in large industrial plants are also more radical and more critical of what the government is doing.[24]

And so the dominant split which was found at the level of the personality in the 1970s, one which caused a fission in identity and widespread opportunism, was transformed into a social cleavage after the experiences of 1980–1.

23. The study referred to on p. 22. n. 17, was replicated on a larger sample and included manual workers and graduate engineers in five large industrial enterprises (see Janicka 1987).
24. It has been proved in many studies (see Adamski, Jasiewicz, Rychard (eds) 1986).

IRENEUSZ BIAŁECKI

What the Poles Thought in 1981

Much has already been said about the causes of the Polish crisis, and many sociological studies have been made of the subject since 1980. In my opinion most of what has been written so far can be classified according to the three prevalent attitudes towards the Polish crisis:

(1) The theory of 'failed expectations'. This attitude can be found in most of what has been said and written to date about the conflict which emerged in August 1980. It involves interpretations which refer to the rapid lowering of material standards after the great leap forward of the 1970s, to the rapid drop in real wages and the emergence of an inflationary surplus. It also includes hypotheses which view the conflict in generational terms, where the aspirations of a generation of young and highly qualified workers and technicians have been blocked. In the sphere of paid employment this occurs through the lack of opportunity for both individual and group promotion as a result of economic stagnation; in the sphere of living conditions this refers, for example, to the housing shortage, which has become increasingly acute. Related to this attitude is a conception concerning the origins of the new 'middle class' which resulted from the similar life and work situations and aspirations of its members. This class was seen as being the bearer of revolt and the driving force of the conflict.

In my view all theories which make reference to so-called excessive or unreasonable demands may be included here. These would be the 'disappointed expectations' of those who are accustomed to receiving goods and services out of proportion with their labour input. In the eyes of society 'what is due' has ceased to bear any relation to 'what one has contributed' as the basis of the creation of

The author is a member of a team within the Polish Academy of Sciences Institute of Philosophy and Sociology, which carried out a public-opinion survey in 1980 and again in 1981, one month before the declaration of martial law.

the common good which is centrally planned and designed for division.

(2) 'The revolt of the powerless.'[1] This attitude is characteristic of those who speak of a blockade of channels for genuine expression and the articulation of interests within the existing structures, particularly members of the Central Council of Trade Unions. Other formulations refer to a 'loss of self-determination' and the resulting alienation of a large section of society; they refer to the protest of those who have no power over the situation in which they must live and work.

(3) A conflict of values. This idea originated against a background of the varying, even antagonistic, value hierarchies espoused by society on the one hand and the authorities on the other. As far as society is concerned, religious and patriotic values were frequently referred to, although there were frequent attempts to co-opt the latter into official ideology. There was also what some saw as the rather anachronistic love of freedom and the greater sensitivity than in other socialist countries towards various forms of constraint. Finally, there are more general and more enigmatic references to Poland's affiliation with European culture, the values of which are seen to be in conflict with the monocentric quasi-totalitarian order currently to be found in Poland. Individualism is probably a specific variant of this opposition; it resists the pre-eminence in central planning which is given to collective as opposed to individual interests.

In popular opinion the individual and his or her autonomy and dignity are values of paramount importance. That is why many people fail to identify with the role ascribed to them in the creation of a better society which is determined in an authoritarian manner and is subject to increasing delay. It is for these very reasons that people are less than sympathetic to the geopolitical reasoning formulated above their heads. It might also be added that such people were troubled by the uncertainty as to whether a centrally planned future should be pursued because it is in fact better or because it is what geopolitical factors demand. Both motives applied simul-

---

1. It would be difficult to mention here all the authors who have written and spoken about the Polish crisis. With regard to the terms which I use to designate the different approaches which have been adopted, I first came across the use of the terms 'failed expectations' and 'middle class' to refer to the Polish context in Kurczewski (1981). Similarly, I first encountered the term 'revolt of the powerless' in an article by Kostecki (1981). The text had earlier been delivered in the form of a lecture.

taneously, as we know, although to some extent they are mutually exclusive.

Finally, there is a more refined version of this conflict of values thesis; this is the theory of a specific dissociation of values in a considerable section of society. According to this theory, the values of society and the authorities are not in precise and exclusive opposition to each other. Rather, they are seen to have co-existed in the minds of citizens and to have created a dualism and dissociation within the 'Polish soul'. Here, the very same people who were opposed to the system within their family circle and among friends, were entangled in various cliques as producers and clients and thus became the allies of the very system they criticised. There was thus a sizeable number of semi-collaborationists and semi-saboteurs with positions of greater or lesser responsibility who sacrificed some values for the sake of others. In large measure their role involved keeping up appearances for the sake of those underneath them and from whose ranks they had emerged, suggesting that they were bargaining and making the most of a bad job. To their superiors they would try to seem as though they were squeezing the maximum cooperation out of the resistant mass below. In recompense for this, such persons received various bonuses and vouchers over and above their wages. This group, or part of it, formed a special kind of no-man's-land between society and the authorities. Here, manners were more gentle, the system of commands and distribution was done away with. It was here that consecutive reforms were blocked.

These are the attitudes which form the context of the Polish crisis. Of course, these categories are neither clear-cut nor mutually exclusive. What these divisions indicate are the particular points of emphasis in explanations which are proffered as to the sources of the conflict and the way in which it developed. Not only is it easy to show that the various categories are not mutually exclusive, in some interpretations they are complementary modes of explanation. For example, the way in which basic needs have failed to be satisfied and the frustration induced by 'failed expectations' has been exacerbated by the blocking of channels which might articulate interests. Existing institutions, particularly the old trade unions, made it impossible for any real negotiations to take place between the representatives of opposing interest groups.

It is also easy to demonstrate that the lack of congruence between 'the centrally planned collective interest' and the demands of society may lead to society losing its capacity for self-determination. However, this may also be the consequence of a conflict between the values held by society on the one hand and the authorities on the other, and may be presented in these terms. This is so, irrespective of whether group interests have been imperfectly planned by the central planner or whether the plan has been imperfect in execution. Society, or rather the greater part of society, prefers to make up its own mind on this question, within different structures and through different institutions.

All three approaches are unanimous in the view that the crisis, however it is described, took the form of a crisis of legitimacy of the authorities. This was confirmed by our survey. In 1981 only about 20 per cent of respondents said they were in favour of the basic principles underlying the model of power relations which had hitherto existed, that is 'the strengthening of the role of the Party' and 'the reinforcement of central planning'. Similarly, it is not at all surprising that belief in these two principles declined during the year between our two surveys. However, there was also a distinct increase in the percentage of persons who expressed some hesitancy, that is in the number of persons who were unsure as to the best way of ruling the country.

It has already been mentioned that the three sets of ideas are not mutually exclusive, and in certain circles they may all be found to co-exist. However, if the authorities declared themselves in favour of one set of ideas over and above the others, this would have important practical implications. For example, if it were assumed that the protests had been caused by the thwarted expectations of a certain category of young qualified workers, an attempt might simply be made to buy some of them off. Indeed, this is an established tactic in dealing with a section of these workers; they have high earnings and are favoured in the allocation of housing. This way out of the crisis might be accompanied by propaganda aimed at lowering aspirations and expectations; for example, 'we cannot distribute what we do not have'.

However, if the crisis were officially seen as the 'revolt of the powerless', this would dictate a rather different strategy for dealing with the crisis. This would involve the development of various forms of self-government which would stimulate and utilise the initiative which had previously been stifled. It would also attempt to relate the interests of various groups to those of the economic system.

The third interpretation offers the worst prospects for emerging from the crisis, although much depends on the definition of value conflict which is assumed. But when one considers the fact that for nearly forty years a considerable section of society has in spite of intense indoctrination held beliefs which contradict the premises of real socialism, it seems reasonable to expect that people will passively resist participation in any proposal to harness individual motivation and initiative to serve the system. In other words, the introduction of the 'Hungarian model' where there is social support for an effective economic system which promotes individual and group enterprise and creates a relatively high standard of living, would be unthinkable in Poland.

What can be said about the interpretations listed above in the light of our survey? First of all, it should be stressed that the survey was merely a poll of public opinion; it did not set out to investigate previously constructed conceptions and interpretations of the Polish crisis. It cannot therefore provide an answer to the question as to which of the three accounts best fits with the actual causes of the crisis. This can only be indirectly inferred, and with difficulty since the interpretations refer to different directions of thinking rather than a set of mutually exclusive competitive hypotheses.

Our survey was carried out in November 1981 and involved a national sample of approximately 1,890 adult persons. Their opinions may be taken as an approximate representation of those held throughout the society. The time during which the investigation was carried out was a crucial one in Poland's history. What then does the survey tell us about social consciousness during this period? In the view of this investigator, three basic points emerged:

(1) Between 60 and 80 per cent of the respondents declared themselves to be in favour of a polycentric power model — that is, the principles of full autonomy of institutions, limited central planning, increased participation of the Church in social life and curtailment of Party rule. Between 7 and 20 per cent of the respondents were against such principles, the exact proportion varying according to the principle in question. The remaining respondents were unclear on this issue.

(2) Some 70 per cent of respondents said they were in favour of the activities of the independent self-governing trade union Solidarity. On the other hand, 14 per cent did not support Solidarity. The remaining respondents did not express one

view or the other.
(3) Between 61 and 84 per cent of the respondents were against
     any reprisals against various forms of political protest. How-
     ever, between 7 and 26 per cent approved of such reprisals,
     while the remainder neither approved nor disapproved.

A rather clear picture emerges from these results. The opinions
which Poles have concerning matters of fundamental importance
differ. There is a boundary line which marks off between 60 and 80
per cent of the respondents from another group of respondents
which never exceeds 20 per cent of the total. The two groups of
respondents thus distinguished, one on each side of our hypothetical dividing line, differ in their position within the power structure.
This boundary may thus be taken to delineate the social sphere of
power. This sphere of power does not necessarily refer to those who
are in authority, nor even those who are in executive positions but
lack actual power. Lower-grade executives are not exactly in authority, but they are much more dependent on authority than are
ordinary employees. There were very few executives with real
authority, if any, among the respondents. The majority of executives taking part in the survey were of lower or middle rank. Thus
the other 20 per cent of respondents were persons who were
subordinate to or dependent on authority rather than having authority themselves.

That is the basic finding of the survey. In the light of this and of
other findings let us now consider the three approaches to the
Polish crisis which were outlined earlier. In my view, the survey
failed to provide support for the 'failed expectations' theory and the
view that the crisis had a predominantly economic basis. Opinions
differed little according to level of income and material circumstances. Moreover, living conditions were not clearly associated
with affiliation to a given trade union — in fact, living conditions
were one of the poorest indicators of opinion. In this respect, job,
education and age were slightly more significant. The best indicator
of opinion was the configuration of trade union affiliation, Party
membership and position occupied. The influence of these characteristics overlapped each other and polarised respondents into those
who were Party and trade union members and who held executive
positions on the one hand, and non-Party Solidarity members in
non-executive positions on the other. However, if we restrict our-
self to a single indicator, then opinions varied most according to

whether respondents were members of Solidarity or of the separate trade unions. Party membership was not such a good indicator of opinion. This shows that the political opinions of the worst off were not essentially different or more radical from those held by the other respondents.

However, deprivation may also be interpreted in relative terms as dissatisfaction caused by excessively high expectations. For instance, the overstimulated aspirations of the younger generation have been frequently referred to in this connection, as have those of better-paid workers and technicians who thought they were entitled to services and privileges which the authorities could not afford. But the results of the survey did not confirm this view either. When asked which problems were most pressing, respondents most frequently referred to questions of housing, food supplies, wages and other matters related to living conditions. Better jobs, promotion and professional training were also occasionally mentioned. Responses to this question most frequently referred to what the respondents thought they could and should have, and the lack of which they keenly resented. Hence the question seemed an effective measure of the extent to which basic needs and aspirations were not satisfied, and of the consequent sense of relative deprivation. And yet views as to which are the 'most pressing problems' fail to differentiate social and political opinion. Nor are they related to trade union affiliation. This also applies to almost the same extent to age and occupation. Young qualified workers are no different from anyone else in the opinions they express, nor did their responses give any indication of a higher level of frustration or dissatisfaction. Thus, even if it is true that revolution is usually brought about by the most privileged sections of the opposing classes — which would seem to be confirmed by the August conflict where young qualified industrial workers were among the most active participants — this was not confirmed by the opinions expressed by this group. This is not to say that the economic crisis of the 1970s widened the hiatus between expectations and the means of satisfying them, or that relative deprivation might have been felt more keenly among some groups than among others during this period. I simply wish to say that these factors failed to have a decisive influence on opinion, nor did they influence trade union affiliation among different categories of respondents. It is quite striking that neither the occupation, age nor education of the respondents gave any indication of the opinions they held. It would thus be rather difficult to distinguish any new 'middle class' on this basis, composed primarily, as some would have it, of young qualified workers and technicians — a class which would be cemented by its keener resentment of failed expectations and by its more radical opinions. Young qualified workers declared themselves to be for pluralism and against monocentrism as often as the remaining respondents. Similarly, they were for Solidarity and reform and against the use of coercive measures to the same extent as the other respondents.

As we mentioned above, the most effective indicator of opinion was a combination of trade union affiliation, position occupied and Party membership — traits which in my view are associated with the amount of power a person has. This would seem to confirm the hypothesis which viewed the crisis as a 'revolt of the powerless', since it is the relation to power which is the most sensitive indicator of opinion. The sense of deprivation and the demands which were made find their most distinct expression along this very boundary line. It should be added that backing for the union authorities referred to political rather than straightforward union matters concerning welfare. It is also noticeable that the respondents here and in other studies gave their strongest support to the national union authorities rather than the regional authorities. Their backing for those whom the respondents themselves elected (e.g. factory committees) was decidedly less strong.

It seems that during the initial stage of the conflict, that is in 1980 and to a lesser degree in 1981, there was a symptomatic divergence between different economic interests and declared opinions on political and social matters. The changes which were called for in the social and economic system were irrelevant, and sometimes even contrary to the respondents' interests as indicated by their living conditions and work situation. To use the dichotomy introduced by Ossowski, ceremonious values prevailed over everyday values. For a time the disinterested ideals of democracy, egalitarian justice where goods are distributed according to need rather than merit, solidarity and unanimous contestation of the existing system, gained ascendancy. These ideals were not directly and immediately related to the material conditions of the respondents' lives. However, the position of the authorities transcended all other social divisions and united opposing camps because there was a universal awareness that it would be impossible to satisfy all interests before self-determination and influence on the course of events had been achieved. This solidarity of attitude and to some extent forced unanimity, and the lack of rootedness in genuine negotiable interests were both the strength and the weakness of the union movement.

Therefore, if one agrees that the course of events was determined by young, relatively well-educated workers of large enterprises, it was neither because their opinions were more radical, nor because their resentment of deprivation was greater than that of others — we are talking here of workers and technicians, not trade union leaders. The influencing factors were more likely to be the conditions under which they worked where communication and organisation were relatively easy, for example the fact that they worked in large groups, in shifts and so on. The vigour of youth and the experience of the protests of 1970 and 1976 probably also played a role.

The third interpretation based on the idea of value conflict would seem to be confirmed by the findings of our survey. The majority of respondents disapproved of the values on which the current system was based. It will be recalled that they were against limiting the role of the Church to religious matters only, against the Party's consolidation of its own role and against an increase in central planning. We might even say that the new type of social system which was called for, was the direct opposite of the existing one. Of course, what we are referring to here is opposition to principles which actually underly actions, not to socialist ideals.

Our survey does not and was not designed to yield information concerning the relation between the approaches enumerated above. To what extent was conflict caused by the opposing values of society and the authorities, and to what extent did it represent the protest of people who lacked self-determination? In other words, if someone demanded more democratic institutional forms through which to achieve his or her aims — that is, forms which are less dictated by central planning and more by religious norms — is this person espousing values which are in opposition to the existing order, or the aspiration for self-realisation, which is also a value, albeit of a different order? Are more democratic institutions an aim in themselves or simply the means through which to realise aspirations which have been determined by tradition? The answer to these questions would seem to depend on the names and labels we give to human aspirations.[2]

2. Let us add by way of digression that this is not simply a terminological or formal question. The opinion is quite frequently expressed that there are suppressed authoritarian and repressive tendencies among a considerable sec-

Our survey is able to provide a specific commentary on the questions formulated above. In the course of a year there was an increase in the number of respondents opting for social principles opposite to those which currently obtained. It is as if the year of stormy events and freedom of expression enabled people to grasp this fact more firmly and express it more unequivocally. Can it be that the year or so of openly evolving conflict brought about a crystallisation and polarisation of beliefs, as well as the renunciation of values which underpinned the former order? If this is the case, it is so despite the fact that confidence in the newly created union movement was somewhat shaken during this time. The conflict of values which was becoming increasingly explicit would then constitute another new form of expression.

---

tion of Polish society. For such people the democratic option would be defined as the negation of the principles of the existing order. Under more 'favourable' circumstances these people would advocate a strong centralised power base to maintain law, order and discipline. In such cases the polycentric option should be included in the category of values which are declared but not espoused, and which are in conflict with more deeply internalised authoritarian tendencies. This would then be yet another way in which the 'Polish soul' is divided.

ANDRZEJ RYCHARD

The Legitimation and Stability of the Social Order in Poland

The chief aim of the chapter is to consider the relationship indicated in the title — that between the legitimation and stability of the social order. I am particularly interested in whether legitimation is a necessary condition of stability or whether the stability of the social order may be achieved by other means. The thesis which I shall attempt to substantiate is that legitimation is in fact not an essential precondition for this stability. For the same reasons, I believe that crises in various types of social order should not automatically be linked with a loss of legitimacy of those in power. Since systems are 'stabilised' by other mechanisms, the lack of legitimacy in itself does not have to result in an immediate loss of stability, in problems of control and in symptoms of crisis. Weber has written that 'submission is not always based on a conviction of legitimacy' (1972: 320). The concept of social order is a wide one with a tradition in sociology. Here I use it in a more narrow sense, however. I am mainly concerned with the institutional dimensions of the legitimation and stability of the social order, that is with the legitimation and stability of a system's basic institutions, particularly those concerned with the exercise of power and their relationship to society. In other words, I focus attention on the sources of the durability of the basic regulators of the 'social order'.

In this I shall make reference to the Polish situation. Concepts such as legitimation and credibility have become extremely popular among sections of the social journalism which has emerged in recent years; they also appear in official usage. Usually, however, this is

This chapter is based on a section of the author's book *Władza i interesy w gospodarce polskiej u Progu lat 80-tych* (Power and interests in the Polish economic system at the beginning of the 1980s), Warsaw: Warsaw University Press 1987. Recent research includes Tarkowski (1986), Pakulski (1986), Staniszkis (1986) and Marody (1986).

unaccompanied by reference to any theoretical concept.[1] In view of this, it seems worth dealing with these questions more systematically. This is also the reason why I shall attempt to place the debates which are taking place in Poland on the issue of legitimation within a wider sociological framework. Without claiming to provide an exhaustive analysis, I am of the opinion that this kind of attempt can contribute to a sociological interpretation of legitimation in Polish society.

Hitherto, discussions have been based on an intuitive understanding of the notion of legitimation. On the whole, it has been taken to be largely synonymous with 'credibility', a belief that the existing social order is a just one. This leads us to consider the possibility that the disagreement between those who support the view that a lack of legitimacy is the main cause of the crisis in Poland and those who do not, is not a matter of the definition of terms. 'Legitimation' can be both broadly and narrowly defined. According to its narrow definition, legitimation would be understood to mean a belief that a system is legitimate, a shared belief in the values which form the basis of the system. Pańków seems to be using this definition when he writes that 'the belief in the legitimacy of the existing power relations, referred to of late as the credibility of the authorities — or more accurately the loss of this belief — seems to be something which touches on the original sources of the crisis of this power system' (1981a: 17).

On the other hand, a wider understanding of the notion of legitimation would not refer to the necessity of common values — it would be less psychological and more sociological. Weber has said that 'from the sociological point of view, the legitimacy of a power system can only be treated as the probability that the proper attitudes will develop to a significant degree and that these ensure appropriate behaviour' (1972: 320). This more behavioural definition identifies legitimate power and effective power; in this sense even totalitarian power may be regarded as legitimate as long as it is effective. However, Weber stated that it was important for the basis of legitimation for power to be treated by citizens as justified, and that this would touch on the matter of 'belief' in legitimacy. Staniszkis, on the other hand, understands power legitimation to involve a principle 'pursuant to which those in power are obeyed without

---

1. With the possible exception of references to Weber's classic differentiation, which is quite often to be found.

recourse to force' (1979: 287). This conceptualisation does not assume the necessity of shared values either.

In what follows I intend to analyse further the distinction between a narrower, more psychological understanding of the concept of legitimation as credibility, and the wider more sociological understanding of the concept. According to the latter, legitimation refers to a principle which orders the system or a mechanism whereby people 'tune into' the system and aspire to certain positions and whereby the system itself acquires identity. I shall deal in turn with questions associated with each of these definitions in order to be able to present my thesis more clearly.

Legitimation as Credibility

Controversy over the role of legitimation in contemporary organisational systems, including political systems, is not an exclusively Polish affair. The view that legitimation is not a necessary condition for a political system to have support has been put forward by Mayntz (1975), who suggested the existence of fundamental factors which influence the general level of support for a political system. Legitimation is one of these factors, as is instrumental motivation, coercion, and *ad hoc* compromises between interest groups. Mayntz maintains that in contemporary societies we are not so much dealing with a crisis in legitimation as a change in the sources of support for political systems. Her opinion has been disputed by Offe (1975), who claims that it is not easy for political systems to discover new sources of support, such as instrumental motivation or the 'management of symbols' suggested by Mayntz. The debate surrounding the phenomenon of 'legitimation crisis' thus allows the Polish issue to be placed within a wider perspective. I shall return to this issue later on.

Mann (1975) has stated that the stability of a system is not so much a question of ideology as of a pragmatic acceptance of one's own place inside the institutional structure. He coins the concept of 'institutional fit' to refer to this non-ideological state of 'tuning into' the system.[2] It seems that the durability of the Polish system is to a considerable degree ensured by a specific set of factors, including

2. Mann writes: 'I am not interested primarily in whether the citizen believes in, private property, but in whether he is factually and stably implicated in it' (1975: 278).

instrumental motivation and 'institutional fit'. One might even formulate a thesis to the effect that one of the main sources of this stability is the peculiar institutional habit which results in adjustment to the existing political and organisational order.[3]

If one keeps to the narrower view which identifies legitimation with the credibility of the authorities, then it would not be valid to state that it was a lack of this credibility which has caused the Polish crises. For example, in my opinion the stability of the Polish social order in 1980 could no longer rest on the foundations on which it had done until then. In particular, the 'calculation motive' (Etzioni 1961) could no longer be set in motion, and it was just this motive which seemed to act as a significant stabilising factor in the 1970s. The consumer aspirations associated with this type of motivation could not be brought into play in view of the imminent economic collapse.

One might be forgiven for wondering why power systems are usually so anxious to prove their legitimacy to society if they are actually obeyed for reasons other than a belief in their legitimacy. The main reason is that the creation of such a belief lends respectability to the authorities. The popularity in official statements of the view that it was a loss of credibility which led to the crisis, is a confirmation of this. The view suggests that the system has always been founded on credibility; the loss of credibility is thus only a temporary phenomenon, not a permanent state. This diagnosis mystifies the real nature of the system and is clearly apologetic. Efforts to construct convincing arguments for the existence of credibility in the narrow sense of legitimation, are doomed to failure since, as Habermas has said, 'there is no administrative production of meaning' (1976: 70). The development of a belief in legitimacy has to be a social process — only then is it effective.

Another distinction has to be drawn. We can speak of legitimation as if it were a real mechanism constructed by society itself; the effect of this mechanism would be that the authorities are 'worthy of being believed'. The concept may, however, also be understood as a set of ideological arguments or techniques applied

3. The distinction between the ideological and pragmatic aspects of legitimation already has a tradition. According to some authors the role of pragmatic mechanisms increases as a new system gains stability, for example Heller's (1982) thesis concerning the 'normalisation' of a system, or the thesis concerning the role of paternalism in legitimation (Feher 1982). Polish authors have also pointed to the importance of pragmatic mechanisms, for example Lamentowicz (1982), Staniszkis (1979), K. Nowak (1984), Wesołowski and Mach (1983) and Morawski (1980).

by the authorities in order to justify their own existence. Power which is not in fact founded on credibility 'produces' complete sets of arguments which are used to legitimise it, primarily in order to gain social respectability.

Such sociological classifications as exist concerning the sources of legitimation of power in socialist systems are usually classifications of techniques used by the authorities, not actual sources of legitimation. Moreover, they do not constitute a typology. Very rarely is there any attempt to link types of legitimation technique with types of power structure or methods of management.

In this connection let us examine the description of legitimation techniques put forward by Lamentowicz (1982). He distinguishes seven types of technique used to legitimise the monopoly of a single political party: (a) reasons connected with the existence of a revolutionary state; (b) doctrine; (c) the historical formula; (d) the sociological formula (the Party being the best representative of workers' interests); (e) 'dialectic' legitimation (only the Party knows how to solve conflicts); and (f) geopolitical legitimation. It can be seen that in distinguishing these analytically interesting 'legitimising' techniques, Lamentowicz does not place them in any order; he does not create a typology. The list can thus be extended; if one goes beyond the justification of the Party's monopoly of power, one can add the manipulation of national symbols or the use of international prestige as important legitimation techniques — Poland being the tenth largest industrial power in the world.

What is significant about these techniques, and possibly our system's method of legitimation in general, is the way they approach the representation and satisfaction of needs and interests. On the whole, the satisfaction of needs is regarded as the basis of legitimation. Pańków (1982b) has drawn attention to this important point by indicating that this is how a specific type of legitimation is constructed — that is, so-called functional legitimation. This has also been commented on by Lamentowicz (1982) and Wiatr (1982). A 'hierarchical representation' of these needs and interests is also assumed. According to this assumption, a higher level, whether within the administration or the Party or the institutional system, represents 'a more general interest' than a lower level. In this way the existence of a centralised power structure is justified.

Markus (1981, 1982) has distinguished overt and covert or negative legitimation techniques in socialist countries. According to her, the authorities make simultaneous reference to two types of legitimation technique: those which belong to official ideology and those which incorporate a mixture of more popular commonsense rules (Markus 1981: 50). Markus observes that this duality leads to an erosion of official ideology. It is possible to point to several forms of covert legitimation technique. Geopolitical legitimation certainly fits this category, and even Lamentowicz, who included it on his list, observes that it is rarely used in a straightforward way. There are also the 'comparative' arguments which point to differences between institutions or power management or 'political climate' in Poland and other socialist countries (Markus 1981: 43). These arguments appeal to emotions which are capable of stabilising the system, and to this extent they are effective. However, they can only 'go public' under specific circumstances, since they do not sit easily with ideological principles as these are propagated in the mass media. It might even be suggested that negative or covert legitimation techniques constitute an acknowledgement of the significance of the problems associated with achieving 'positive' legitimation. This is the very reason why these techniques are only used under specific circumstances.

Staniszkis (1979) has made one of the few efforts to create a typology in this area, in her attempt to link legitimation techniques and leadership techniques. However, her initial thesis is open to question in my view. She states that existing means for the construction of legitimation determine the leadership techniques which are available. The opposite seems closer to the truth. The origins of the socialist system in Poland show that first there was a certain leadership and management structure, and only subsequently was there any attempt to legitimise it. This does not diminish the value of significant parts of Staniszkis' thesis which shows the changes traditional legitimation (in Weber's sense) has gone through in contemporary Poland. The kind of legitimation which is applied in administrative activities, according to the author, possesses certain features of traditional legitimation such as the inheritance of organisational status, a narrow range of formalisation at higher levels, management by exception and the myth of unity. At the same time there have been significant modifications, for example, the future and not the past acts as a source of legitimation, as does the belief in the lack of any alternative, rather than the fact that the authorities have always existed.

These distinctions, particularly Markus's distinction between overt and covert legitimation, can serve as the basis for the construction of a wider typology. A suitable starting-point for this endeavour would be the question as to whether some legitimation techniques are used more frequently with regard to some social groups than to others. That is, are legitimising arguments 'sociological and differentiating'? The hypothesis might be advanced, for example, that under certain circumstances covert techniques are used more frequently than overt techniques with regard to particular groups. This question would be worth empirical investigation. Such investigation would be focused on two issues. First, when the system appeals to the representatives of various groups, what values and interests does it invoke? Secondly, what types of legitimation technique can be counted on to win the acceptance of these groups?[4] It would be particularly interesting to consider how the issue of the interdependence between political legitimation and economic efficiency is viewed in public opinion. For example, to what degree does the achievement of political credibility result in the acceptance of economic non-efficiency? Or does economic efficiency and the satisfaction of material needs give rise to consent to a lack of political legitimation (see Pacewicz 1983)? How do these issues vary according to social group? The answers to these questions could be used in the construction of an empirically grounded typology of legitimation techniques.

As long as legitimation arguments are 'techniques' — that is, conscious goal-orientated behaviour — they are in essence contradictory to true legitimation which has its roots in spontaneity. To put it simply, we may say that legitimation is a particular property of the system which is 'handed over' to those in power by society and never *vice versa*. This means that a political system can never create the foundations of legitimation for itself, it has to receive them from society.

However, this does not mean that a social order whose institutions are not regarded as credible cannot be stable. As I have already mentioned, there are other sources of the stability of a social order. The image of political power as a force which has to be regarded as legitimate by citizens in order to be effective and durable is wishful thinking and as such is of limited descriptive and explanatory value. A crisis of credibility does not have to be the cause of a crisis in power relations, and it was not the cause of the crisis in Poland at the beginning of the 1980s.

4. Compare this, for example, with Lamentowicz (1982).

The fact that following August 1980 the issue of the gaining, and not the regaining, of legitimacy by the authorities started to be seen as the only way of getting out of the crisis, is another matter altogether. There were no economic stabilising factors which could be set in motion, and the political climate did not seem conducive to the use of coercion as a means of regaining stability. Perhaps there was also a fear that coercion would be ineffective. For these reasons there were in the post-August period certain observable attempts on the part of society to gain legitimation. I refer to this as social legitimation since it could only have been initiated by society.

These attempts were reflected in suggestions which embodied the idea of a 'social contract', but were unsuccessful. An analysis of the reasons for this failure is beyond the scope of a single chapter. Suffice it to say that in my opinion the reasons should not be seen as mistakes or false moves by either or both of the potential parties to such a contract. Rather, there should be an examination of the structural conditions necessary for such attempts to be successful. One such condition is the acceptance of a view of the system which includes the significant disparity of interests between social groups and the power structure. It is obviously an essential precondition of any contract that there should exist 'parties', that is partners with equal rights. Ideological factors (e.g. the myth that those in power represent social interests) may act as an obstacle to this condition, as may pragmatic factors. The latter result from the anxiety that the efficiency of organisational systems and of the economy in particular would decline were these systems to become the arena for the resolution of contradictory interests. At the root of these doubts lies the conviction that congruence of interests is a precondition for efficiency in complex organisational systems. Although there is empirical evidence to contradict this view, it is firmly ensconced in the consciousness of management and large sections of society. In practice, the entire management system is founded on this assumption.

Another structural reason for the failure to establish a social contract, one which was no less important than that mentioned above, was the fear of both parties — that is, the Party-state apparatus and Solidarity — that they would lose their identity as a result of signing the contract.[5] These two significant factors by no means exhaust the issue.

5. I am basing my argument on Bialer's (1983) thesis, according to which one should also examine 'whose' legitimation (i.e. legitimation in which sections of society) is most important for the system.

The dramatic turn of events which took place on 13 December 1981 placed in a new light the question of legitimation in the sense of credibility. The mass mobilisation of the means of coercion gave rise to the impression that this was the main stabiliser of the social order. At the same time declarations were made by representatives of the official structures which revealed a conviction that there was almost no social acceptance and that it was necessary at that stage to lean on chosen groups. Thus minority legitimation arguments were constructed. The hypothesis may be put forward that on a mass scale the main emphasis was on the control of behaviour, although a variety of attitudes was tolerated.[6] Do these facts support the view that credibility was being abandoned as a 'soft' source of stability (e.g. in permitting a variety of attitudes), with increasing dependence on 'hard' stabilising factors such as behaviour control and coercion? It is difficult to answer a question posed in these general terms, especially since there has been a simultaneous development of PRON-type institutions (see p. 19, n. 14) and the symbols of national agreement are still in currency.

In my view the question as to whether the signs of an abandoning of mass credibility indicate a temporary or permanent change is a key one for understanding the nature of the social order. It may be assumed, because of the difficulty in fitting the principle of minority legitimation into the ideology, that this is a temporary mechanism.

It should be noted, however, that although legitimation had new propaganda aspects following 13 December 1981, it still exhibited the same permanent systemic features — that is, its importance as a source of stability rather than credibility.

We now turn to the effect on legitimation of the official lifting of martial law in July 1983, the elections of June 1984 and finally the amnesty of July 1984. From the moment martial law was declared the stability of the system was maintained by the significant divergence between the relative conformism of behaviour and radicalism of attitudes. This resulted from the fact that in Poland under martial law it would have been difficult to predict behaviour on the basis of attitudes. The converse was also true. The inconsistency between attitudes and behaviour persisted beyond the lifting of

6. The following quotation from a periodical is a vivid illustration of this point: 'At present the objective of our policy with regard to the younger generation ought to be the neutralisation of the majority and the activation of a minority only. . . . If they don't want to be red at present, let them be green, let us channel their energy into private enterprise, the building of family homes or the founding of communities' (Klakson 1982).

martial law and led to interesting phenomena during the June elections in 1984. The relatively high turn-out — 75 per cent according to official sources — prompted the authorities to gradually discard the minority legitimation arguments which had proved ideologically inconvenient. The outcome of the elections was officially interpreted as an expression of political support which allowed the authorities to speak of 'majority' legitimation. This was evident in the statements of the government spokesman who said that no-one could now accuse those in power of having imposed themselves on society. From the point of view of the thesis presented here, the authorities were making a typical mistake; they were making extrapolations with regard to political support (i.e. attitudes) on the basis of conformist behaviour during the elections. This was not sound reasoning, but it allowed the use of the election argument to justify the amnesty. But there were other more important reasons, such as the expectation that restrictions imposed by the West would be relaxed. The official interpretation of electoral turn-out as an expression of conscious political support inclines one to the view that for ideological and doctrinal reasons we are witnessing a return to the phraseology and myth of mass support. A more realistic picture of the system as depending on coercion and other stabilising factors beyond legitimation is giving way to a less realistic picture of a system which is accepted by the masses. Although the picture is less realistic, it is ideologically more acceptable for the other Communist countries.

Legitimation as the Identity of a Social Order

In this section I wish to return to the basic distinction which was drawn at the beginning of the chapter between legitimation as credibility and a wider understanding where legitimation might be taken to mean a socially accepted principle defining the system's identity. This principle incorporates the notion of credibility in a sense, for it has to be socially accepted. But in addition to this aspect of the notion, legitimation may be taken to exist as an objective mechanism which ensures that people are incorporated into the system's institutions, thus motivating them to occupy certain positions. 'Individual success' is a good example of a principle which helped create the identity of early capitalism. If the concept of legitimation is understood in this wider sense, then I believe that

45

the thesis which views legitimation as a source of system stability holds.[7] What is involved here is a certain fundamental principle which 'identifies' the system. The interesting question is to discover this 'identity principle', or in other words, what is it that legitimates in the wider sense the type of social order which exists in Poland?

In what follows I shall put forward the view that no single principle or unified set of principles exists as such. Thus there is a sense in which the social order does not have its own identity but embodies contradictory principles. As a result it is possible to speak of a permanent crisis of legitimation. The perspective adopted here allows the consideration of the Polish case to be placed within the framework of a more general debate on the crisis of legitimation which is taking place in the West, and with which the names of Jurgen Habermas and Claus Offe have been associated, although the latter does not use the term 'legitimation crisis'.

The description of the Polish situation as one of 'legitimation crisis' which has been so frequent in the press and even in the academic world, usually makes no reference to sociological tradition. To my knowledge, the only exception is the use of certain concepts coined by Habermas in the interpretation of research findings concerning the value systems of local politicians (Jasińska and Siemieńska 1981; Jasińska 1984). Let us then consider the implications of applying concepts of legitimation and crisis of legitimation developed by Western scholars, to the Polish situation. According to Habermas, a legitimation crisis is caused by the fact that in order to maintain the market and the relations of production, state intervention is necessary. This contradicts the normative basis of capitalism and the individualism which is the source of legitimation for capitalism.[8] Therefore the source of the legitimation crisis lies in the fact that the distribution of the social product takes place according to political criteria (see Kaniowski 1976). State intervention has to be justified and it is here that there is a danger of a legitimation crisis. This is a simplified version of Habermas's general idea. For him, a crisis of legitimation is but one in a series of

7. As I have already mentioned, the controversy between Mayntz and Offe over the role played by legitimation in the stabilisation of a political system — where Offe opposes Mayntz's view that it is easy to find reasons for a system's permanence other than legitimacy — seems in large part to stem from the 'narrower' definition of legitimation used by Mayntz and the wider one used by Offe (1975: 257).

8. Habermas has written that the 'legitimation crisis . . . results from the fact that the fulfilment of government planning tasks places in question the structure of the depoliticized public realm and thereby the formally democratic securing of the private autonomous disposition of the means of production' (1976: 46).

crises in the economic, rational and motivational spheres. In addition, the crisis of legitimation is contained within a wider framework of the crisis phenomenon in general. Thus it may be interpreted as a consequence of certain control problems in the integration of a system's social institutions. Habermas starts off with a system approach to crisis as a state where 'the structure of the social system allows fewer possibilities for problem-solving than are necessary to the continued existence of the system' (Habermas 1976: 2). He modifies this notion, calling attention to the disintegration of social institutions as a necessary precondition of crisis. Continuing in this way, he reaches a definition where control problems cause a crisis 'if (and only if) they cannot be resolved within the range of possibility that is circumscribed by the organisational principle of the society' (Habermas 1976: 6). This principle in turn limits the scope of change which can take place within a system without a disruption of identity. That is why crises are linked to a system's loss of identity as a result of problems of control. The legitimation crisis is also one of identity: in order to maintain capitalism, a control problem, it is necessary for the state to intervene, thus damaging the identity of a system based on individualism.

Claus Offe follows a similar line of reasoning when he points to the contradictions which exist between effectiveness and legitimation. He states that it is possible to maintain the goods-product relations of production only through 'non-product' means, that is through state intervention. This involved potential problems for legitimation (Offe 1975: 253).

If one accepts that a legitimation crisis is caused by state intervention to maintain the capitalist system, then by force of the same reasoning one can say that there is currently an inverse legitimation crisis in Poland. The situation here is that in order to maintain a socialist state and thus to maintain political control over social life, it is necessary to apply methods derived from the operation of market forces. In general outline the crisis is the same; to maintain the order, methods have to be used which contradict that order. Viewed in this way, it can be said that there has been a crisis of legitimation in Poland throughout her postwar history. The same pattern was invariably used, whether it was the economic reforms where market elements were implanted into a centrally managed system, or political reforms where democratising elements were introduced into a non-democratic structure. And the pattern was such that alien elements were actually introduced into the same structure. It can be said, therefore, that the socialist system has not developed methods of overcoming economic and political difficult-ies which are socialist in essence. It has always been a case of applying means which were foreign to the socialist practice of the time in politics and economics. No other methods existed. Crises thus touch upon the issue of a system's identity; they allow us to ask at what point the system ceases to be the same system. The decisions which were taken at the end of 1981 show that in the eyes of the control centre this boundary occurs at the point where the system's institutional structure is threatened, particularly the power of a single centre and political control over the economy. This institutional stability appears to be even more important than the stability of ideal principles for the simple reason that the identity principles have not been completely formulated in ideological language. The role played by the institutional structure as the chief stabilising structure which gives a system its 'identity' gives us a better understanding of what was said earlier on the subject of credibility. I quoted Mann's view that it is not the acceptance of ideological principles (i.e. credibility) which acts as the source of system stability. In his view it is the institutional fit, the tuning into a system — that is, a certain pragmatic acceptance of institutions and not principles — which is the main stabilising factor. If institu-tional fit is the main factor responsible for the stability of a system, then the perceived violation of this institutional structure is a signal that this stability is under threat.

However, it should not be forgotten that the restoration of one of the identity principles — that is, the role of the official institutional structures — remains in contradiction to the other identity prin-ciples of the system. As a result of this restoration, the system gains institutional legitimation, as measured by the degree to which it is accepted by its allies and the extent of its compatibility with the institutions of real socialism — but it does not gain social legit-imation. What is involved here is the non-compatibility of the system's identity principles. An institutional structure characteristic of a strong monocentric power centre for the political management of the economy sits side by side a more or less formal set of principles and institutions typical of a parliamentary democracy, civil rights and a goods-finance economy. Some of these are merely decorative, others, such as the goods-finance economy, have a rather more tangible existence.

The feature which these latter institutions share is the fact that they are descended from the earlier system which was abolished by the 'socialist revolution'. They are socially accepted and may even be the source of unrealistic hope, as in the case of the market economy. They form the foundation of everyday life and are the source of social aspirations.[9] The historical origins of these institutions are not of primary importance for social consciousness; more important is the conviction that these are in a sense the universal attributes of modern societies, attributes which such societies cannot do without. Ideologically, some of them have at times been treated as 'relics of capitalism', but since they are socially accepted, they provide the sole basis for the construction of the social legitimation of the system. These are the system's other identity principles, and they are often in conflict with those discussed earlier.

It is possible to say that the system does not have a cohesive basis for legitimation. On the one hand, a high level of centralisation and the importance of political power in determining economic activity are the constitutive principles of the system's identity. The introduction of spontaneous mechanisms into politics and market mechanisms into the economy may be viewed as a violation of these identity principles, thus causing a legitimation crisis. Hence the legitimation crisis is inverse in relation to that which occurs under capitalism. This is a crisis of institutional legitimation understood as a deviation from the principles of real socialism. But this is the way of achieving social legitimation in the sense of the compatibility of the system's principles and mechanisms with social aspirations.

On the other hand, though, actions which are intended to endow the system with the identity of 'real socialism' and the re-establishment of institutional legitimation, preclude social legitimation.

This idea is an elaboration of the notion of the conflict of identity principles and system legitimation when the reinforcement of the centralist principle impairs the market principle and *vice versa* (Rychard 1983: 112–13). This distinction is analogous to that drawn by Kamiński (1983: 139–40; 1984: 221–2) between two forms of equilibrium: that of the institutional system and that which exists 'between the material and non-material products of the system and the needs and aspirations of society' (1984: 221). In his opinion one

9. Attempts to construct the so-called 'socialist way of life' indicate that at least some of the advocates of the system's ideology consider such a state of affairs to be an embarrassment.

49

kind of equilibrium upsets the other. To express this in the terms of the argument put forward above, one might say that the existence of the two types of equilibrium is linked to the lack of cohesive system identity. Like Kamiński, I am of the view that this can give rise to problems connected to the reformability of the system, although the lack of a cohesive identity may offer hope for reform inasmuch as the flexibility of the system's identity may make it uncertain at what point the system has lost this identity.[10]

Due to the lack of a coherent basis for legitimation, the system is in a state of permanent legitimation crisis. The two basic identity principles — one accepting the role of the centre and the other allowing for spontaneous and market mechanisms — are opposed to each other. This has two rather pessimistic implications. On the one hand, each time attempts are made to achieve social legitimation there will be a threat to the authorities of a loss of institutional legitimation. In other words, the achievement of identity by society does not go hand in hand with the achievement of identity by the power system.

Having distinguished these two types of principles implicated in the identity of the system and the two mutually contradictory sources of legitimation (social and institutional) associated with these principles, we are now able to put forward the view that legitimation crisis is a permanent feature of the system. If we accept this view, then the debate concerning the causes of the crisis and the causes of the loss of credibility are placed in a new perspective. These arguments embody the assumption that there is something which 'causes' crises and their cyclical recurrence, and hence that crises are a deviation from a normal state. This in turn means that crises are seen as 'problems to be solved in a scientific way'. The perceived need for technical knowledge to resolve crises, mystifies them; they appear as a kind of intellectual riddle — all that has to be done is to find an intelligent solution. The point of this mystification is to conceal the political nature of the crises, including legitimation crises, and to ignore the fact that in order for them to be resolved, it is necessary to modify the political structure of the system.

But if we adopt the approach advocated here, it is not possible to find an answer to the question as to the causes of the crisis. The

10. This lack of a cohesive identity breeds a greater lack of cohesiveness, and even conflict with regard to the legitimation techniques which are used. See, for example, Markus and Brunner (1982).

crisis is a structural feature which is implicated in the very essence of the system. This is particularly true of the identity crisis, and hence the crisis of legitimation. It is of course possible to show that these identity principles are not consistent under capitalism either, and that under capitalism they also result in a crisis of legitimation. Such arguments have been put forward by Offe (1975: 254), for example. But under these circumstances legitimation crisis is associated with changes in the nature of capitalism — an increase in state intervention — while in our case, identity crisis is associated with permanent features of the power structure.

Social inequality is a good area for analysing the legitimation crisis in an empirically controlled manner. As is known, social inequality is legitimated in the same way in socialist and capitalist doctrine. The socialist principle 'to each according to his work' is identical to the Western achievement principle according to which people's rewards are a function of their labour input. Both Western and Polish authors have drawn attention to this similarity (Ossowski 1968: 185; Lane 1976: 178). According to Offe (1976), this principle does not function in the West, since level of income is becoming increasingly detached from level of labour input and more determined by political factors. This gives rise to problems connected with the legitimation of inequalities, and as a result is one of the causes of a legitimation crisis. Since the phrase 'to each according to his work' is also an element in one of the Polish system's identity principles, both on the level of axiology and on the level of social consciousness, any deviations from the principle will also give rise to problems in legitimating social inequalities. These deviations are nevertheless significant and are frequently mentioned in the literature (Wesołowski 1974: 208; Kruczkowska 1979; Rychard 1981). The principle has a limited sphere of operation for many reasons. For example, it is limited by political factors, where the alternative principle 'to each according to his usefulness to the authorities' comes into play (Sikorska, Rychard and Wnuk-Lipiński 1982). In this case we are dealing with a legitimation crisis which is similar to that described in the Western literature since the basis of the violated principle is the same.

It is clear, then, that the normative basis of socialism is inconsistent with the means used to legitimate the social order in Poland. As a result, all actions can be interpreted as a violation of the basis of legitimation and hence the system's identity; an increase in state intervention and the central regulation of incomes undermines the principle 'to each according to his work', while the introduction of consistent market mechanisms undermines the legitimation of 'real socialism'. This example illustrates the difficulties associated with the legitimation of social inequalities and indicates a possible direction for an empirical analysis of the subject.

Conclusion

In this chapter I have argued that legitimation defined as the credibility of the authorities is not and never has been a necessary condition for the stability of the system in Poland. To summarise, it may be stated that stability was achieved by means of a specific combination of coercion or the fear of it, instrumental motives and 'institutional habits' resulting from negative comparisons and a sense of no alternative. It can be argued that different elements of this stabilising mixture were of varying importance at different points in time. They certainly varied in potency according to class or social stratum. Thus legitimation in the sense of credibility was not a factor which stabilised the system, for this credibility has been absent and in its absence other mechanisms have acted as stabilisers. The situation has been one of permanent credibility crisis.

If legitimation is taken in a wider sense to mean a principle of the system's identity, then there is also a permanent legitimation crisis. However, this crisis lies in the fact that the system's identity principles contradict each other. On the whole the credibility crisis is of little significance to the authorities and for their stability; the second affects the very core of the system. The way in which the authorities read these principles of identity gives empirical meaning to the argument concerning reform and reformability.

The definition of legitimation as the identity of a system paves the way for empirical studies. It is possible to discover social attitudes towards these identity principles, particularly since some of these principles are encapsulated in slogans calling for social justice and hence are the focus of emotions. It is for this reason that our perspective is useful for studies of social inequalities and divergences of interest. Apart from allowing attitudes towards axiological principles to be examined, it also allows one to discover the degree to which the fundamental institutions of real socialism are accepted or rejected. The success of a system's legitimation is best studied by analysing attitudes to real institutions, not just to abstract slogans.

JADWIGA STANISZKIS

The Political Articulation of Property Rights: Some Reflections on the 'Inert Structure'

The Economic Decline

I shall be concerned here with two basic problems: the state of Polish society following the 'beautiful disease' of 1980–1, and the dilemmas faced by the government during the economic decline of the system known as 'real socialism'. I will show how these two problems are closely interrelated by highlighting how the phenomenon of 'inert structure' influenced the rebellion of 1980–1.

The Polish situation and also, less obviously, that in other countries of the 'socialist camp' would suggest that the driving forces of the economy under what is known as real socialism, are on the decline. Under these conditions the economy has two specific characteristics. In the first place, there is the nature of property rights — conceived of as sanctioned human interactions relating to limited resources, and access to them means that property is non-exclusive since multiple subjects enjoy various and ambiguous rights to the same assets which are non-transferable on the capital market and non-inheritable (Furbotn and Pejovich, n.d.). What I am referring to is of course state property or what some call national property. Secondly, the state plays a special role not only by substituting itself for economic mechanisms — for example, by transferring funds between sectors as a substitute for accumulation or by creating demand or by setting prices — but also by systematically redistributing the costs and profits of production by administrative measures.[1]

1. The amount allocated from the national budget to the economy is a fair indication of the state's redistributive actions. In 1982 such allocations amounted to 655 billion złoty, equivalent to one-third of the budget. In 1983 planned allocations

Because of the specific nature of the property rights of the state and the way it redistributes assets, individual and social utilities and costs are often widely divergent, with ramified consequences for efficiency and innovation (see North and Thomas 1973). This divergence between social benefits and profits on the one hand, and individual benefits on the other, is reinforced by a lack of economic mechanisms and the consequent arbitrary measures of the effects of economic activities.

The utility of a person's productive work in the state sector in terms of remuneration depends on how the effects of his or her labour are rated and on the image of efficiency transmitted to the bosses rather than on real economic results.[2] On the other hand, the state can shift the costs of economic activity from one state-owned enterprise to another, thus increasing still further the discrepancy between individual utility and social benefit. Some economic entities receive more than their relative contribution since many state-owned enterprises are not charged with the full costs of their operation and thus tend to be wasteful.[3]

It is just this built-in discrepancy between individual utility and social benefit which distinguishes real socialism from capitalism. Under socialism, human needs are the same as under capitalism, but they are transformed into interests and objectives which, in contrast to the capitalist case, do not require rational behaviour for their fulfilment. This is because of the nature of the decision-making structure, which is in turn defined by the character of property rights and the role of the state in the economy. This discrepancy holds at the level of the individual only, for at the level of society the cleavage between economically rational behaviour and need satisfaction leads to less fulfilment of all needs than would have been the case with the same initial resources but different property relations. The lack of rationality in economic behaviour is best seen in the case of investment. In economies based on private property, investment

---

were to be equal to one-half of the budget. Whatever the economic situation, redistribution and excessive pay-outs have always been a substitute for accumulation in real socialism.

2. Conventionalisation of effects has made it possible to pay out bonuses amounting to 300 billion złoty at the end of 1982, while the value of production surplus only amounted to 100 billion.

3. The performance of the state and cooperative sectors of the economy in 1982 may serve as an example of the way cost externalisation increases as property becomes less exclusive. In the case of the state sector, both production and efficiency fell (output fell by 2 per cent), but as a result of price manipulation it achieved greater profitability than the cooperative sector, where production increased by 4.2 per cent and efficiency by 9.9 per cent.

means spending one's own resources, whereas under real socialism resources are assigned to an enterprise by the state, which is redistributing resources which have been taken from someone else. Investment therefore becomes appropriation rather than spending, and because of the bonuses which are associated with it, it is also a specific kind of consumption.[4]

Another consequence of the systemic peculiarities of real socialism which have been mentioned above is the fact that decision situations differ from those in systems based on exclusive, inheritable and marketable capital. I do not intend to reiterate the thesis that 'politics has the upper hand over the economy'. What I will show is the specific logical structure of decision situations in the real socialist economy. This may be observed on three levels.

In the first place, with the property rights of real socialism there is no market as there is under capitalism and hence there is no universal and reliable standard by which to measure economic outcomes. Decisions cannot fail therefore to be arbitrary. Such factors in decision-making as cost or profit cannot be objectified, because in the absence of a market they remain empty terms. Real socialism has substituted universal government control over material processes for the universal abstract rules regulating the transfer of capital. Totalisation of social life has been substituted for self-regulation. This centralised and detailed control results in the organisational segmentation of the economy. This not only inhibits production; thus incurring efficiency costs, it also increases overall transaction costs. These costs are in any case higher than under capitalism where the exclusivity of property rights, and the limited externalisation of costs and profits means that the least violence or pressure warranted by the rationality of exchange, can be applied to enforce contracts. In sum, it may be seen from looking at the analytical model alone, although this has also had empirical confirmation, that under real socialism decisions are of necessity more arbitrary. In addition, in order to make the economy work, much greater force must be applied than under systems based on exclusive, hereditary and marketable property.

Secondly, neither the specific nature of the relations of production under real socialism nor the specific nature of decision-making processes can be understood without considering the ideological foundations of the state. These foundations consist on the one hand

4. This was pointed out by Strzelecki (1983).

of a system of *a priori* logic where not only objectives but the means used to achieve these objectives, are evaluated in doctrinal rather than empirical terms. Further, they involve a notion of legality which is defined in material rather than formal terms whereby the power elite considers its own interests to be *the* social interest — the last remnants of the idea of the *avant-garde*. Here the law is treated as a versatile instrument of the administration and not as a regulator of social life which binds together the rulers and the ruled and is formulated under the control of the latter, or at least independently of the executive. Since the means used to attain social objectives are not neutral, and as they are selected *a priori* as we mentioned above, it is not possible to apply experimental principles, as when all possible methods are equal at the outset and choices are made between them only in terms of economic efficiency. Instead, a hierarchy of independently evaluated factors emerges, some of which operate in symbolic and empirically unverifiable ways.

The third characteristic of economic decision-making processes under real socialism is the lack of those systemic conditions required for formal rationality and which according to Weber (1922: 48–60) are responsible for the economic efficiency, innovativeness and dynamism of the capitalist system. It will be recalled that such conditions include: (a) the calculability of actions and comparability of their effects, something which is impossible under socialism as we mentioned above; (b) the existence of exclusive property which implies responsibility; and (c) the specific structural conflict caused by the exploitation and/or innovation which is part of the process of accumulation. The parties involved in this conflict, including the working class, gain more in this situation than their counterparts under real socialism. This is because of socialism's externalisation of costs and benefits, its substitution of central redistribution for accumulation in the name of social equity, its indirect exploitation and inert structure — all of which results in very low economic efficiency. These last two factors will be dealt with in more detail later on.

All these structural features of the decision-making process under real socialism, which are caused by the structural properties of the system, not only result in lower economic efficiency, they also imply a hierarchical structure, an arbitrariness of solutions, and a large measure of control and coercion in social life. This is shown by an analysis of the consequences of the specific nature of socialist relations of production, including the nature of property rights.

For the time being we shall not consider the role of political doctrine and the one-party system which is to reinforce the hierarchical, coercive and arbitrary tendencies we have mentioned. As has been observed, the innovative and efficient use of the forces of production is only possible when individual and macroeconomic rationalities are not widely discrepant. Where the gap between them is great, as it is under real socialism, there can only be extensive development. That is to say, the economy can only develop as long as there are untapped resources which can be called on. However, when there are no active economic mechanisms, and particularly where there is no capital market providing a universal regulating standard, there arises a systemic incapacity for the rational allocation of resources. Under real socialism, problems of allocation are solved by administrative decision, and by leaps and bounds as it were, for the recurrent recessions necessitate extraordinary decisions for reallocation of funds so that the self-defeating logic of the system may be temporarily blocked. These phenomena are a regular consequence of the constitutive characteristics of the system. In the past the recurrent recessions performed not only a regulatory function, they also revitalised the system by temporarily lowering tensions and in this way allowed the system to survive basically unchanged.

The latest Polish crisis is different, however. The Polish economic system bears all the hallmarks of real socialism, and has hitherto developed in an autarkic-symbiotic manner.[5] But because of its very nature — the role of the state in the economy and the nature of property relations — it has turned out to be unable to make the transition to an intensive economy or to pay its debts. Moreover, now that its extensive reserves have been exhausted, it has clearly lost all capacity for growth and by itself cannot even maintain levels already achieved. Although it is still able to survive politically, the system seems to have reached a dead end as far as the economy is concerned. Symptomatic of this state of affairs is the increasing

---

5. The autarkic-symbiotic industrialisation model typical of economies in real socialism is marked by an initial rapid extensive development under conditions of demand created by the state, the transfer of resources between sectors in place of accumulation and an isolated regional market (Comecon). The result is a permanently imbalanced structure and a lack of competitiveness with Western economies. During the subsequent phases of industrialisation, a system-induced lack of innovation leads to the transfer of Western technology and the creation of credit barriers. In this situation the dependence on the import of components from the West leads to a sharp brake on growth, permanent stagnation and new closure within the less demanding Comecon market.

bankruptcy of the state, which cannot repay its internal and external debts,[6] the breakdown of the ability to accumulate capital, petrification of a dysfunctional capital structure caused by bad investment policies, rapid decapitalisation as permanent assets fail to be regenerated, and material barriers to further extensive growth (see Krzak 1983). In addition, there are two further elements which should be taken into account. The current fiscal crisis has set in train certain processes which prejudice capital reconstruction even further, and secondly the economy is rapidly becoming segmented into isolated markets and pseudo-markets by proliferating regulations. It might be noted that these symptoms are strikingly similar to the circumstances associated with the downfall of another system based on extensive growth machanisms (Weber 1976).

Theoretically, the reaction to this exhaustion of a system based on a specific form of property ought to involve a change in the nature of this property. In the case of real socialism, however, this is impossible and not only for ideological reasons. The costs of a transformation to different property relations, for example the reintroduction of exclusive and marketable capital property, appear too high, both for the authorities and for society; this is a theme to which I will return when dealing with the 'inert structure' phenomenon. A more probable reaction, and one which is already visible, is the tendency of the state to do away with those exclusive property rights which still exist in Poland, particularly if they pertain to resources which are in short supply. An example of this is the compulsory labour of so-called 'social parasites'. It should be emphasised here that all the economic reforms undertaken hitherto under real socialism in Poland and elsewhere have been limited to shifts of responsibility within non-exclusive property forms while the principle of non-exclusivity itself has remained intact. The hereditary and marketable property of capital could not be introduced for the obvious reason that this would mean a change of the system itself. Thus even where reforms have gone some way towards market exchange — as in Hungary, or towards self-government in industry — as in Yugoslavia, they have failed to reconcile individual and

---

6. At the end of 1982, 68.5 per cent of the loans made by credit institutions were financed by foreign sources, private savings and income from the non-state sector of the economy. In the same year only 3.8 per cent of finance for development was provided by the state as owner of the means of production. The economy and investment were thus financed by sources outside the state-owned economy. See Wierzbicki (1983).

social utility to the degree typical of private property systems.

Not only have exclusive property rights been restricted, but there has also been a nervous search for a political mode of survival during what promises to be either a permanent state of stagnation or possibly slight progress in quantitative terms coupled with permanent structural regression in both production and consumption. Two aspects of this model have begun to emerge, and in a surrealist way they resemble choices which were made in Poland at the turn of 1947.

First of all, there has been a resurgence of some features of the totalitarian phase of the system which were later rejected as it evolved towards the authoritarian-bureaucratic formula. This evolution was marked by a progressive ritualisation of ideology and by the loss of the politically specific role of the Party. The Party had been losing its identity due to the *nomenklatura* system and the overlapping of hierarchies until it not only lost its central role in the decision-making process after 13 December 1981, but the lack of a formula role turned out to be a trap from which it could not escape. At low and middle levels particularly, the barrier of imagination which in the past meant that it was inconceivable that something not be referred to 'the secretary' (i.e. the local party boss), broke down. First the commissars arrived, and now decisions are taken by the administration in conjunction with the military and the security services. Another tendency in this process was the abandonment of the totalitarian ideal of mobilisation so characteristic of the late 1940s and early 1950s in Poland and of the early 1920s in the Soviet Union. This was marked by a blurring of the distinction between the apparatus of repression and the so-called masses because of the existence of specific forms of control from below.

Although the Communist Party has not regained its role, the authorities are obviously returning to ideology. However, this is a selective process. For example, the policy of cooperation with the Church and the use of Church influence to stabilise the system, has been continued. The return to the *a priori* language of ideology seems to be less an expression of faith than of despair. It is an attempt to give some meaning to the activities of the establishment when this is becoming more and more problematic. Moreover, in this period of decline, the control function of ideology seems to have become particularly important for Moscow. Since it considers all reform to be destabilising, it has probably decided to introduce more stringent integration controls within its camp. The establishment of each country is of course subject to such control. By pressurising them through the orthodox groups within each party to use the language of ideology, the available alternative solutions are carried out; many solutions cannot be expressed in this language. The language of ideology also determines ways of defining situations and problems. This is why there has been a remarkable increase of ideological pressure upon the power establishments throughout the socialist camp. Paradoxically, this return to the language of ideology by the ruling elites, including General Jaruzelski's government, which used to emphasise its non-ideological stance and avoid class rhetoric, does not automatically entail an increase in the political significance of orthodox groups within parties which have been criticising these elites for the rejection of ideology in practice.

Other signs of a return to totalitarian techniques include attempts to reactivate anti-hierarchical mechanisms of control and to selectively mobilise society from above through the organisation of activist conferences and youth round-ups while maintaining de-mobilising pressure on all genuine forms of collective activity. This kind of pressure was characteristic of the totalitarian regime in its later bureaucratic phase. Recent legislation shows that demobilisation is proceeding apace. The fact that the authoritarian-bureaucratic phase has been abandoned is evidenced by the package of legislation introduced by the Seym on 21 July 1983. The legislation is consistent in barring any possible reconstruction of corporate structures which would articulate interests and negotiate with the government. Such structures used to exist during the 1970s, and it seems that only this kind of imperfect elitist pluralism is compatible with the one-party system. In the 1970s there were artists' and professional associations and learned societies which represented the interests of respective corporate groups and negotiated with the authorities on a range of subjects including social issues which were functionally related to their specific concerns. This did not represent a threat to the authorities, since no political demands were made. The advantage of this arrangement for the Party was that it derived some kind of legitimation from the fact that socially respected groups approached it with their demands. This was significant for an organisation which, in spite of its 'leading role', seemed to suffer from a complex of its own legal ambiguity in the power system. The price paid for the emergence of a corporate network of interest articulation was rapidly increasing tension among middle-ranking members of the power apparatus. This was due to the selective and informal exemption from control of some areas of activity which were not felt to be threatening to the establishment; for example, certain 'outspoken' conferences were allowed to take place. In order for this demoralising game to be played at all, the petitioners had to have credibility and therefore had to be allowed to gain status and prestige. It is the destabilisation which this and related tensions in the executive apparatus led to which has prompted the recent legal changes. This indicate that those presently in power are afraid of any activisation of society, even if this were to take the controlled and elitist form of the 1970s. The bill of 21 July is highly reminiscent of the Czar's counter-reform measures of 1880. There, too, the politicisation and attempted coordination of corporate structures brought about legislation as a result of which they ceased to be self-governing organisations. As in present-day Poland, the governors received broad executive prerogatives. The Czar considered the attempts of corporate groups to break away from their vested-interest status and to collaborate with, for example, working-class organisations, to be particularly menacing.[7]

The retreat from authoritarian bureaucratism is the first visible feature of political survival during the economic decline of the system. The second facet of this mode of survival is tight integration within Comecon.

The choice in 1947–8 of the Soviet model of industrialisation meant decapitalisation of the private sector, and particularly agriculture, as a substitute for accumulation. This, together with the creation of demand by the state and the autarky within the socialist camp has been responsible for an unbalanced and self-suffocating economic structure. Transactions with the rational economies of the West, although extremely difficult, were still possible, particularly in view of the fact that the West was interested in such transactions and was likely to offer credit. Moreover, during the six-year plan genuine economic growth was achieved. But this was growth without development, and social needs were not met as well as they would have been had different property relations and a different industrialisation model prevailed. Current integration within the socialist camp and the Comecon-wide search for further extensive reserves can no longer yield substantial growth. At best, it may stabilise stagnation at its present level and prevent further deterioration. The price of

7. A detailed analysis of the 'counter-reform' can be found in Jaśkiewicz (1979).

the process, however, is higher than it was thirty years ago. It will involve the structural degradation of each national economy, since there will be a decrease in the complexity and variety of economic structures of production and consumption, a permanent severance of contacts with the West and closure within non-innovative systems. Indeed, this degradation, which will probably be permanent, will prevent a return to even the present low level of exchange with the West.

Integration also means the monopoly of contacts with the West by Moscow. In addition, there will be greater and more permanent dependence on the Soviet Union than before.

The principles according to which Comecon operates and the logic of the industrialisation model which has been imposed on Poland, can be interpreted as the colonialisation of countries with a higher level of economic development by a country which is more politically powerful but economically less developed. By imposing specific economic structures and the rules by which the game is played, it has reduced the colonialised countries to its own level and made them dependent on its resources. The Hungarians are currently engaged in a lonely struggle to reform Comecon since they are aware what reintegration based on non-market principles means. The Romanians have lowered their level of consumption and taken draconian measures in an attempt to restructure their economy so that it will be independent of Comecon. However, their radically centralistic methods offer no chance of success, and the sacrifices of Romanian society will be in vain. Because of the political weakness of its power elite, Poland is for the time being accepting the least favourable 'integrative' economic solutions — for example, in producing consumer goods for its neighbours using raw materials supplied by them. The terms of this trade remain highly unfavourable to Poland, although they have improved in recent years.

Both the return to the language of ideology and integration within the socialist block can be analysed as symptoms of the tightening of control throughout the socialist camp. This is not the first time that the logistic reserves of the system, including the use of violence as a factor in production, have been called upon in Eastern Europe. I am referring to the refeudalisation which took place between the fifteenth and seventeenth centuries and the return to serfdom in a situation of crisis which included a crisis of economic exchange with the West. It might be instructive for an understanding of reactions to the current crisis to analyse the structural and political factors behind these events. For in spite of the short-term economic benefits which they brought, there was a general civilisational regression, while in the West the cities became the centres of economic development, more exclusive forms of property were assumed and political transformations took place.

Ideology as Logical Reserve?

The logical end of the system in terms of its economic rationality does not mean its demise in historical terms, as I have emphasised. Moreover, we can imagine a set of objectives which might create a logical reserve for the system. The necessity of attaining these objectives would involve highlighting certain fields of activity for which the system is better fitted than systems based on different forms of property and power.

In the first place, the system is still able to redistribute commodities quickly, using administrative means; in a crisis situation it can rapidly redistribute the costs of its own inefficiency. Secondly, centres of political power have practically unlimited opportunity for intervening in production, including the weak private property sector. Thirdly, the state can still do much to indoctrinate society and to isolate it from outside influences. Finally, the authorities still have extensive means for repression at their disposal; this includes coercion in production, for example through the militarisation of enterprise.

The capacity for rapid mobilisation of resources specific to state forms of property has lost its significance as the reserves necessary for extensive growth have been exhausted.

These domains of activity may be moulded by ideological directives. Thus it is possible to talk of a 'class' redistribution of the costs of the crisis or 'class' repression instead of bureaucratic or indiscriminate repression. It is also possible to revert to a totalitarian Utopia in the field of culture and education. Ideology seems to be a quite indispensable element in the logical reserves of the system.

The ruling group in Poland may choose to put these reserves to one of several uses; that is to say, it may reformulate the system's objectives in one or another way. This will not solve the real problems or increase the amount of goods in short supply, but it may lend some meaning to the activities of the establishment, at

63

least in the eyes of the apparatus and a section of society; the establishment is thus protected against the charge of ideological indifference. This is particularly important for Jaruzelski's government. The legitimating formula which it expounded at the outset of martial law was 'repression and reform', or repression in order to implement reform. As long as this government believed in its own mission, it was able to stave off the assaults of the orthodox faction in the Party apparatus. At present, however, when hopes of economic reform seem increasingly faint,[8] Jaruzelski's team seems psychologically and politically too weak to limit itself to mere survival forms of control and repression in order to disarm society. They need a frame of reference to lend significance to its actions; the previous training of the members of this team and the diminishing room for manoeuvre makes a return to ideological justification quite natural. A content analysis of a variety of conferences, documents, speeches and publications during recent months reveal four variants of logical reserves:

(1) Redistribution of the costs of the crisis within production. Here it is suggested that financial burdens such as profit tax or 'inflation tax' be shared by subjects with similar incomes, depending on how 'socialist' each economic sector is. By charging state employees less and private businesses more, thus depriving private business of capital resources, the crisis could be used to accelerate revolutionary progress towards socialism.[9] The superiority of state property over any other form of property is argued in *a priori* abstract terms which are immune to empirical evidence. Because it is reluctant to apply this kind of logic to its actions, General Jaruzelski's regime has been criticised openly, although no names have been mentioned. Kurowicki has used the Leninist charge of 'objectivism' in his attacks. An 'objectivist' is a politician who has not only lost his 'class' perspective but who is also unable to 'carry out revolution as an art' and who does not understand that 'politics is creation'. Objectivists become slaves to facts, 'recognising their logic as infallible and unchanging. The only thing they can do is to adjust to the circumstances. They neither think nor act dialectically. Their knowledge about the system is the knowledge of a servant, functionally subservient to individual interest'.[10]

8. Arguments which show that the reform has failed are to be found in Skir (n.d.).
9. See the discussion in *Polityka*, 1983, no. 11, especially the article by J. Kurowicki.
10. Lenin's definition from the paper 'The Economic Substance of Narodnik

The implementation of the idea of 'accelerated revolution', while redistributing the costs of the crisis, means of course a further decrease in economic efficiency and further curbs on enterprise and initiative in the name of *a priori* logic. The so-called 'second economy' — small-scale unrecorded business, trade and services — which sometimes makes use of state-owned equipment and reprocessed materials and plays on regional differences in prices and demand, would probably decline. This economy yields no direct profit to the state but improves market supply. In Hungary it is the second economy, and more thrifty use of extensive development reserves due to the early introduction of reforms, which is responsible for the fact that the economic situation is better in that country than elsewhere in the block. Jaruzelski's government is probably aware of the costs of implementing the 'revolutionary' variant. This is why, in spite of strong pressure, attempts have been made to keep private sector profits off the record until 1984, although taxes are to be raised before that date. However, voices raised at a conference of 'working-class activists' held in Warsaw in March 1983 demanded earlier action by the Ministry of Finance in recording and controlling private business assets.

(2) Redistribution of the costs of the crisis in consumption. This variant is less permeated by the abstract dialectical logic of Marxist orthodoxy, but puts strong emphasis on its popular egalitarian message. This was the approach accepted by the conference of 'working-class activists' which had been set up but not fully controlled by the Jaruzelski government. There are two options open here. One is the imposition of heavy taxation on so-called luxury goods, starting with carpets. Although this strategy has the strong support of the working-class rank and file of the Party, it is limited by the self-interest of the power apparatus. If redistributive emotions were to be excessively aroused, as when groups of workers check the incomes of the administration or search apartments looking for spare rooms, the ruling group is likely to suffer. Nevertheless, such attempts have actually been made.

The other option here is the placing of limits on collective consumption, for example the withdrawal of budgetary financing of prescriptions, the introduction of charges for food in sanatoriums, lower sickness benefits for the first three days off work and so on. Decisions like these, some of which have already been implemented,

---

Ideology' is discussed by Kurowicki (1983: 25ff.).

are subject to severe criticism on the part of workers and Party rank and file who say that such moves do away with the welfare achievements of socialism.

(3) The third variant may be referred to as the 'lyrical' model of totalitarian Utopia, which calls for further attempts to construct a new socialist culture, a new man and a new morality. Here it is admitted that it was a mistake to compete with the West in the past in the field of consumption, because in this respect any system based on state property is doomed. Advocates of this approach call for priority to be given to objectives such as an equitable distribution of goods or upward 'class' mobility promoted by the state, for which the socialist system is better fitted than is capitalism (Gulczyński 1982). A classical example of this kind of longing for the unambiguity of fully controlled, closed societies devoid of state-independent property may be found in Marx's *Grundrisse*. According to Marx, the logic of such societies means, among other things, that they will not evolve needs which they might not be able to satisfy. They are 'more sublime than the modern world wherever we are looking for a closed whole, for a form with given limits. Such a world is fulfilment on a limited plane, whereas the modern world leaves us dissatisfied' (Marx 1966: 16).[11] The radicalism of the imagination in this excerpt, with its longing for purity of form and cohesiveness of the system and its objectives, is, I believe, very dangerous. Traces of this kind of radicalism can be found in Poland today as the search for the system's logical reserves continues.

I referred to this variant as 'lyrical' because it deals only with aims, and not with the methods which are to be used to achieve these aims. It attempts to conceal the inevitable coercion involved in such a sudden reorientation of aspirations. For it would mean the isolation of society from Western 'consumerism', repression of those who espouse Western values and styles, administrative selection in cultural matters, the importance of political and 'class' criteria for promotion and, finally, the administrative redistribution of material goods.

This variant is distinguished from the others in that it fails to consider the methods which will be used to achieve the desired objectives. In the other variants, the means are as important, if not more so, than the ends. For example, in the first variant mentioned

---

11. We can hardly assume that the quotation is ironical. More probably it expresses fascination with the rationality of control.

above, the decapitalisation of the private sector, the subordination of the law to the interests of the 'direct producers' and the subordination of ethics to the 'class struggle' were the means to the 'class redistribution of the costs of the crisis'. It was hoped in this way not only to accelerate the construction of Communism but also to purify the Party of 'objectivists', since the workers were opposed to the 'liberal petty bourgeois' defending 'abstract moral norms' (Kurowicki 1983: 28, 32, 39). This approach is based on the material idea of legal equity which has no use for the formal letter of the law. This is a trend which emerged during the Solidarity period. The specific methods of the second variant promoted the importance of mobilisation for totalitarian Utopia. An extra bonus for the power elite is the inevitable fear which accompanies the definition of a crime in flexible terms rather than according to the letter of the law. The selective application of this principle to representatives of the administration and the power apparatus would be an extra instrument of control and provide public opinion with scapegoats from time to time.

(4) The final way of lending significance to the activities of the authorities relates to the 'class' rather than chaotic bureaucratic character of repression. The postulate of class repression was first formulated in leaflets produced by the 'Working-Class Platform', which expressed the views of one faction within the Party apparatus. A crackdown on the 'petty bourgeois inspirators of counter-revolution' (i.e. certain circles of the intelligentsia) is proposed. Those within the power elite who are said to protect these groups are also attacked. Purges of personnel in academic and cultural institutions are demanded. Jaruzelski's government would still probably rather not adopt this variant, preferring more subtle methods to outright repression.[12] On the other hand, it is increasingly heard in speeches that they resent the failure of these intelligentsia groups to appreciate the efforts which have allegedly been made to protect them. Moreover, always prone to overestimate Polish intellectuals' mental prowess, they present the intelligentsia's refusal to cooperate not only as symbolic action but as sabotage in that the authorities are deprived of possible solutions which could be found in cabinets of experts. This belief may finally induce Jaruzelski's government to apply 'class' repression. This would have a major advantage from the point of view of the ruling group: it would provide those in

12. Cf. the polemics between St Kwiatkowski in 'O opozycji i własnych błędach' (The opposition and our own faults), *Tu i Teraz*, no. 10, and T. Wrbicka in *Trybuna Ludu*, 1983, nos. 64 and 80.

charge of coercion with 'ennobling' ideological rationalisations. There are those who believe that the victims, too, suffer less when the system of repression is clear, non-selective and, in its own awkward way, logical.

Whatever the extent to which any or all of these variants may be ultimately implemented, a return to ideological orthodoxy and violence as the instrument for achieving this, seems inevitable. In all probability it will end up with the ideological structuring and rationalisation of the mode of repression. The redistribution of the costs of the crisis in the productive sphere is suicidal; in the field of consumption it is incompatible with the self-interest of the power apparatus. The lyrical model of totalitarian Utopia is not only hard to achieve, it cannot produce the rapid results its advocates expect.

All these processes, including the return to ideological orthodoxy and the use of violence as a factor in production, indicate that a new variety of totalism is on the way in. On the one hand, the situation now is very different from that in the early 1950s; actions are taken in cold blood, they are dictated by logic rather than faith or emotions, and the context is one of permanent stagnation rather than rapid extensive development and mass upward mobility. But there are surrealistic similarities too, for example in the preparation of the bill on the national councils (*rady narodowe*) in 1950, and currently of the new version, an unchanged philosophy of power can be discerned.[13]

This totalism is being implemented by people who would probably prefer to see an authoritarian, bureaucratic and ideologically neutral regime in Poland, accompanied by economic reforms. However, as I have already indicated, they neither have the political muscle nor the psychological tenacity to remain within the limits of the politics of day-to-day survival. In any case this would by no means make them popular, and they would be distanced from the ultimate weapon of ideology which might afford them protection from the assaults of the apparatus.

The common stereotypes of Stalinism and of totalism in general are based on an image of a strong oppressive state and omnipresent ideological pressure. However, an analysis of Stalinism in Poland as well as the Soviet Union suggests a different picture. In particular, two important elements are missing from these stereotypes. In the

13. Underlying the discussion of this bill was the thesis that democratisation means decentralisation of responsibility within the state, but definitely does not include making local self-government independent of the state.

first place, the borderline between the apparatus of repression and society has always been a fluid one; the so-called masses have been broadly involved in repression, and society has always exercised self-control. Secondly, ideological pressure has been channelled in two streams. The executive power apparatus and the so-called activists have been inculcated with a particular propaganda and with *a priori*, empirically unverifiable logical arguments rationalising obedience; at the same time the general public was subjected to quite different propaganda techniques.

Both of these elements are absent from the commonsense stereotypes which are now making a come-back. For example, the Special Commissions for Orderly Conduct recently set up by the Council of Ministers[14] — that is, by the government, for it is the bureaucracy and not the Party apparatus which is implementing totalism this time — had as its task the pursual and prosecution of actions which were formally legal but incompatible with 'the spirit of the law' or ideological formulas. The aim of their activities was to create fear since anything could be construed as a criminal act, and also to encourage self-control on the part of society. This self-control had two aspects. In the first place, the activities of the Commissions were directed against managerial staff and members of executive boards, who would also be responsible for the 'criminal' deeds of their subordinates; this reinforced stringent control along the lines defined by the Commissions. Secondly, workers were encouraged to become members of these Commissions. Paradoxically, in this the central bureaucracy was taking advantage of the anti-bureaucratic attitudes and resentment of the workers while appealing to such values as egalitarianism. This calculated move to involve workers in repressive activities is based on faith in the power of the destruction of hierarchies. It is assumed that the attraction of attacking one's superiors and getting away with it would have a magic appeal, as was the case in the 1950s. If we add sheer envy and personal vindictiveness to the picture, we obtain what Gross (1982) has referred to as a typical technique of totalism, the 'privatisation of repression'.

Again, the kind of pressure exerted by propaganda on the

14. The bill of the Council of Ministers creating the Special Conduct Commissions came into force on 18 February 1983 (DZ. U., no. 8, para. 41). When martial law was lifted these Commissions were also abolished, and the tasks they dealt with taken over by local administration and the appropriate minister. This indicates that this version of selective mobilisation has been abandoned, probably because it was unsuccessful.

executive power apparatus and on the masses is the same in that in both cases there is an attempt to segment consciousness, that is to imprint information which cannot be verified from the individual's empirical perspective. However, this information varies at every level, according to who is the object of the propaganda. Thus the ruling apparatus is informed of the facts in a relatively reliable manner, for access to information is a kind of privilege. However, the propaganda at the same time inculcates the *a priori* logic of dialectical reasoning which is impervious to facts and leads to conclusions which are convenient for the system. What is surprising is the continuous nature of propaganda pressure. Even during the Ninth Communist Party Congress in July 1981, when there was a marked effort on the part of the Party to adjust to the new situation, and when elections to the new Central Committee were more or less democratic, all the basic documents emanating from the Congress were composed of the same elements as the propaganda from the period of the most intense totalism. The dialectical logic behind this reasoning rationalises obedience and is based on a number of assumptions.

The first of these is that the 'objective' or true interests of the working class are not congruent with its 'empirical' awareness or 'potential' consciousness. According to this tenet, the Party may be defending the interests of the workers even when it is acting against them.

The second assumption is based on a mixture of 'progressiveness' which is immune to empirical evidence, and of abstract principle legitimising political decisions and impervious to facts. It is on the basis of the authority of theory and not of experience that the first of these ingredients defines which form of social life is superior and which inferior. For example, monism is better than pluralism in the articulation of interests; state ownership is more 'progressive' than individual, corporate or communal ownership. The second ingredient is according to General Jaruzelski's much repeated formula that 'history will show that we were right'. This relieves one from the necessity of taking public opinion into account, since history overrides actual social life and current expressions of social consciousness.

The third assumption is the specific or Hegelian conception of the crisis, and was in much evidence in the documents from the Ninth Congress. Here the main cause of Poland's crisis is 'the imperfect embodiment of socialism'. In other words, what exists is explained in terms of what does not. The main conflicts of the system are explained away in a similar manner. What they really are, are conflicts between theory and reality.[15] This approach has several merits in propaganda terms: (a) it does away with the necessity to analyse real life and the use of the notion of conflict of interests; (b) the responsibility of the power apparatus is diluted; (c) the idea of socialism is itself protected, since it is only mentioned in the context of what is 'missing'. In this way, ideology remains invulnerable to the crisis and confident of its own structure and assumptions.

This framework for thinking about reality not only allows the apparatus to maintain an unchanged vision and unchanged arguments in spite of the turns taken by history, they also facilitate adjustment to new demands from above. This is what indoctrination is all about as far as the executive apparatus of power is concerned.

The situation changes when we look at the propaganda aimed at people at large. Here there are four discernible elements:

(1) The propaganda purposefully insults the feelings of those exposed to it, for example in what it says about Solidarity or when it contradicts obvious facts. It is not its task to convince anyone. What it aims to do is to demonstrate the imperative character of social relations, or to put it more plainly, to show that the authorities can afford to insult society.

(2) On another plane, the propaganda aims to clog up minds by creating a stream of empirically unverifiable noise. This task is performed by certain types of propositional structure such as those which pre-empt or neutralise possible resistance in the audience by using double negations, for example: 'It is not true that the reform has failed'. Verbless propositions might be used, such as 'The youth with the Party', leaving the audience to surmise whether the verb is 'is', 'should be', or whatever. Again, positive phenomena are coupled with the use of proper nouns such as 'everyone', 'most people' and,

15. The draft programme for the Ninth Congress of the Communist Party (Założenia programowe na IX Zjazd PZPR), Warsaw, 1981, mentioned the following main lines of conflict; that between the principles of socialism and their implementation; that between what is said and what is done; and that between aspirations and opportunities (Part I, thesis 3). The 'idea of socialism' was seen to be the main area of conflict, with the Party defending the idea and its enemies attacking it (Part II, thesis 8). The programme stated that 'the current crisis was not a crisis of socialist principles, but a consequence of having ignored them'. A detailed analysis of these documents can be found in Łazarski (1982).

conversely, negative phenomena are qualified by the use of words such as 'sometimes' or 'a few'. Such formulas as 'more and more' and 'still' also have a jamming effect.

(3) The propaganda often attempts to transmit definite information with reference to status space. Following the experience of August 1980, the authorities are well aware of the importance status competition had for Solidarity members. An example of this kind of information is the phrase which has come into recent usage: 'The Party has got off its knees'.

(4) Finally, the propaganda exploits the fundamentalist attitude common among working-class members of Solidarity whereby the strength of one's actions depends on the conviction of the moral rightness of one's case. The propaganda thus aims to create feelings of guilt in society, for example for the economic crisis, which is presented as resulting exclusively from the strikes during the Solidarity period, or by propagating gossip about the alleged embezzlements perpetrated by union leaders. It would appear that the visit of John Paul II has effectively defused any such guilt feelings while reinforcing fundamentalist attitudes — the formula that good shall prevail over evil. It should be stressed that the fundamentalist attitude has dynamics of its own. Essentially, it cannot be altered by persuasion, it can only be destroyed through demobilisation and an erosion of its moral basis.

The authorities' search for the system's logical reserves and the slow evolution towards a new version of totalism is not taking place in a social void. It is impossible to understand current social consciousness in Poland without analysing the phenomenon of 'inert structure', which is a consequence of the way the economy works under real socialism.

The Paradoxes of Revolt within the 'Inert Structure'

The 'inert structure' is a characteristic of systems based on non-individualised, non-hereditary and non-marketable property, usually state property, supplemented by a weak private sector whose opportunities for accumulation and exchange are subject to administrative check. Another characteristic of such systems, as we mentioned above, is the substitution of state intervention for economic mechanisms. Both features have serious consequences for social structure. In the inert structure, interests are formal and abstract since there are no neutral centres of gravity determined by active economic mechanisms. Moreover, the way in which needs are fulfilled depends largely on the organisation of management and on the redistributive decisions of the state. The ability to manipulate tensions and to defend the welfare of certain groups further prevent a sharp polarisation of interests. In this kind of structure exploitation takes indirect forms. Unlike capitalists, the bureaucrats who manage the means of production do not have to be innovative or able to exploit employees more in order to survive. Under socialism, where we often have centrally controlled distribution or transfers of budget allocations between sectors (e.g. from agriculture to industry), there are no classical bearers of economic rationality. In this kind of system, exploitation is not the result of a strong motive to accumulate — this kind of motive only arises in the distribution of national income, not in production — but stems rather from the systemic inefficiency of allocation and utilisation of forces of production, the costs of this being borne by the whole society. The phenomenon of indirect exploitation and the manipulation of tensions by the state strengthens the view that interests within the state economy are conventional. Moreover, in those enterprises where conventionalisation of effects and externalisation of costs acts in favour of the employees at the expense of the rest of society, all employees, regardless of their position in the hierarchy, are interested in the maintainance of these mechanisms even though they contribute to the efficiency of the system as a whole. This awkward 'community' of interests linked with their conventionality makes conflicts in the inert structure extremely ambiguous; they are usually played out in different areas from industrial conflicts in the West.

However, the most striking feature of the inert structure is the unconscious reinforcement of opposite poles when opponents are interested in the maintainance of the inner logic of the system. Thus, although they are in conflict, they regenerate on various levels and by various means the system's constitutive mechanism of redistribution. In addition, neither of the two opposing sides in the inert structure — the political authorities and civil society — who are tied together in a fashion through the principle of non-exclusive property, wish to set the structure in motion by introducing any active economic mechanisms. The authorities are afraid of political destabilisation, while society is afraid of the costs involved, in terms of rapid diversification, objectivisation of the depth of the crisis and the localised concentration of some of its effects. The fact that in the inert structure, 'nobody fights their battles until the end', can sometimes be a luxury, especially for economically weaker groups, for the state interferes with and limits the logic of particular roles in the economy as soon as there is a threat of too much polarisation or too much pauperisation, that is of political destabilisation.[16] Security is another luxury, as there is no competition or struggle; there is the 'satisfaction' of equality since everyone is equally dependent on the political authorities. The lifelessness of the social structure is an index of the extent to which society has been sequestered by the state; it is what the authorities bank on when they hope for the stabilisation of the system.

In this inert structure, ideas concerning the main lines of conflict are remarkably incoherent. The prevalent view of social conflicts is that they are rather static, while in actuality interests are contrived and unstable, since tensions are shifted by administrative manipulation and superimposed upon these conflicts are the effects of the community of interests described above. However, it is the idea people have concerning the nature of conflicts, rather than the real structure of interests, which determine actions. One conflict which has gone unperceived is that which exists between all state employees on the one hand and the private sector (e.g. agriculture) on the other. This conflict stems from differences in the nature of rationality in each case, the specific nature of accumulation under socialism, and also from the effects of the policy of the destruction of money and hence the market, through state sector handouts which bear no relation to the economic effects of work. The bi-polar view of the conflict between state and society is reinforced by the clash of interests between state functionaries and other members of society concerning the level of funding required to maintain a repressive state.

The weakness of horizontal links and the underdevelopment of civil society typical of state economies, or the development of civil society around different moral visions and value systems, as is

16. This is a formulation taken from a work by P. Milukov entitled *Ocherki po istorii russkoy kultury*, Petersburg, 1909. It deals with a system based on weak dependent land ownership where land is given in return for services to the state. The land is under the simultaneous ownership of the Czar, landlord and the rural serf community. The 'society of service' described by Milukov has much in common with the inert structure described here.

happening in Poland today, give rise to artificiality and theatricality in public life, even at those rare moments when society wins an opportunity to speak about itself. At such moments and under the impact of the perception of real interests, there can also be observed the rapid corrosion of all attempts to integrate around values. If one adds to this the fact that the opposing parties tend to support each other, we can imagine the schizoid and ambiguous social atmosphere surrounding these climaxes. All this means that coalitions built on normative visions of society are volatile and waves of protest are liable to suddenly subside as they oscillate between ecstasy and resentment.

The complexity and ambiguity of crises in statist systems is additionally linked to the fact that in such crises opposition usually involves society's unified defiance of the state. But this is an abstract opposition: on the one hand society and the state are interwoven, while on the other they are linked by the innumerable ties of non-exclusive property. Thus, while polarisation is very strongly felt, it is paradoxically very difficult to trace the actual divisions. In a system of non-exclusive property the most extensive rights are at the top level of the state authorities. Other rights exist at the level of the enterprises, but no-one can claim the right to inherit or to sell his or her own fraction of the means of production. Non-exclusive property belongs to everyone and to no-one. There are still large areas of common interest — that is, common to everyone whose interests lie in maintaining cost externalisation. There also remains the whole ambiguity of the inert structure. All these factors confuse the picture of actual social conflict. Society's internal divisions, for example those related to one's position in the division of labour, do not influence positions adopted in a conflict situation, especially when this conflict is highly generalised and polarised, but they do determine the ways in which the conflict situation is experienced.

All these paradoxes become conspicuous in a situation of revolt such as occurred in Poland in August 1980. This is something the authorities have been aware of and have been trying to use to their own advantage. One of the basic reasons why paradoxes emerged was the fact that the process which was initiated in August and extended over the whole Solidarity period took place on three often incompatible levels. First, this process represented genuine, fundamentalist, working-class rebellion, as the term is understood by Camus in *The Rebel*. It was a deep moral experience and simultaneously a time for learning about oneself and the world. These two elements together made the first phase of the August events a kind of non-aggressive holiday. The shared experience of the strikes was a lesson in itself for the strikers, as well as allowing them to discover dignity and solidarity in themselves. Moral values thus became categories through which reality was experienced. That is to say, the workers began to think of society in terms of moral categories. This distinguished them from the educated class for whom moral values are categories about which one thinks in terms of other abstract concepts which are already available. These moral values were often the first general concepts the workers had ever encountered which allowed them to navigate alone in the waters of large-scale social processes. In this sense, the August rebellion was primarily a cultural revolution which radically changed the workers' ontological perspective. These new moral standards not only served as ways of evaluating phenomena but also reorientated perception, focusing attention on certain phenomena and defining them in relation to each other. Thus, moral values served as cognitive categories and as such functioned as unchanging and unanalysable entities invulnerable to further operationalisation or compromise. What radical fundamentalism is essentially about is the rejection of politics as a means of solving problems. Compromise, the essence of politics, is regarded as morally unacceptable; it also involves the translation into the language of institutions of values which are stringent, irreducible and inflexible — not because of what the fundamentalist believes but because of the functions performed by these values in the cognitive perception of the world and in orientating oneself in social space.

The joyful first stage of the rebellion involved an act of cognition and an affirmation of a newly discovered self in the world of values. Emotions oscillated between claims that the values discovered in rebellion be recognised, particularly by the authorities, and the desire to withdraw and play safe within one's own 'independent' organisation, the independence of which was measured by lack of contact with the other side. This attitude, however, underwent further transformations. The experience of values and the cognitive changes which went with it had been made possible by participation in the movement. Very soon, however, it was no longer the values themselves but the interests of the movement which formed the basis for imposing order on the world and defining what would be the object of attention. In the process, the holiday atmosphere gave way to feelings of threat, while the need for affirmation was transformed into aggressivity.

Finally, in the third phase which took place in the autumn of 1981, the interests of the Solidarity Union were synthesised into the single dimension of the status of the movement *vis-à-vis* other institutions, especially the Communist Party. The status of the movement now became not only the standard according to which the world was apprehended, but a means to its transformation — as when Party organisations were expelled from enterprises.

On another level, the August process revealed the hallmark of the inert structure, as for example when egalitarian demands were addressed to the state as the agent responsible for redistributing goods, and substituting for economic mechanisms. Instead, it is in such roles that the state makes the system's inert structure permanent. Other effects of the inert structure also appeared, for example the incompatibility between the way in which alliances and conflicts were perceived as based on solidarity, and the actual bargaining which was taking place between different corporate groups.

At a third and final level the movement was articulated according to how the crisis was experienced by the educated class. As a result of their different position within the division of labour, they experience the world differently and have different linguistic competences and cognitive perspective from the workers. August 1980 was a deep moral and emotional experience for the Polish intelligentsia too, but it was not the fusion of both moral and cognitive experience that it was for the workers. While moral values represented categories of thought for the workers, for the intelligentsia they were the object of thought. The intelligentsia not only differed from the workers in the lesser degree of fundamentalism which they evinced; the primary distinction between them lay in the fact that for the workers the August experience was a process of self-discovery while for the educated class it represented a discovery of politics. However, it was the experience of the latter which came through in accounts of what Solidarity was about. What was missing from the texts and programmes which emerged was the commonality of working-class experience with its authoritarian undertones, and their lack of political commitment; politics seemed too narrow to express the joy of discovering the world and the self. The texts did not deal with the crisis by analysing the inner dynamics of socialism, but tended to interpret the current state of affairs in terms of the lack of liberal-democratic institutions in the superstructure. The working-class experience of the rebellion involved a liberation from cognitive chaos, a sense of community and fundamentalism interwoven with radicalism of statuses — and the traps of the inert structure. If this experience could have been satisfactorily expressed, perhaps the Polish August could have made a greater impact on the imagination of other nations. As it is, the movement has had to wear the strait-jacket of liberal culture and, as a result, its populist and millenary character has been camouflaged. The documents of the movement have failed to show how moral experience was able to become a cognitive approach to the world. Since it has not received expression, this aspect of the Polish August is slowly sinking into oblivion.

The failure to fully grasp what has happened and how the transition from liberation to confrontation occurred, the deep grudge against the authorities which they have failed to recognise or the deliberate falsification of the affirmative motive of the movement, the destruction of the standards which for a short time offered an orientation for social life and the return of chaos — these are only a few of the characteristics of working-class attitude at the time of writing, on the third anniversary of August. Associated with this is a subtle but clear resentment against the educated class. The impact of the inert structure is felt in the demands for an equitable distribution of the costs of the crisis. Also detectable is an apathy which is associated with the specific dynamics of the fundamentalist attitude. This passivity and bewilderment not only have to do with the fear of repression. Other significant factors are the erosion of the certainty of moral rightness and the loss of innocence, as when we remained silent when people were dying after 13 December 1981, and the destruction of the oversimplified myth that an independent organisation of their own is all the Poles need for their problems to vanish. The specific dynamics of fundamentalism, from the euphoria experienced from ordering the world according to moral standards to a kind of paralysis where all activity within formal structures, including activity of a critical nature, is regarded as collaboration, are an extra asset for the authorities in their attempts to totally demobilise society. Such passivity would appear incompatible with the spectacular marches which were seen during the Pope's visit to Poland, or before that, during the May Day rallies. But readiness for isolated, partly ritualised and relatively safe expressive acts ('Here we are, just out of Mass . . .') should not be confused with long-term purposeful action which calls for people to think in depth about the relevant issues. This can only be achieved through participation in formal structures. It seems to me that this is what is necessary for the future, even if the price is the erosion of the fundamentalism so characteristic of Solidarity, so beautiful but so politically dangerous. This was also my view a year ago when I proposed winning over the new unions and making as much use as possible of all existing associations and organisations. However, recent legislation has cast doubt over the adoption of such tactics.

While the economic decline still leaves quite open the possibility of political survival and continues to block opportunities to transform the constitutive features of real socialism — that is, non-exclusive, non-hereditary and non-marketable capital property — it is the first dimension of the Polish drama. It should be emphasised that the impediments to transformation stem not only from the dogmas and interests of the ruling group but also from society's inert structure. The second dimension of the drama is represented by the dilemmas of political articulation which are visible even in situations of revolt and which have been described above. The source of such dilemmas is the fundamentalism of attitudes and, again, the inert structure.

WITOLD MORAWSKI

Self-management and Economic Reform

Worker Self-management 1956–8

Discussions concerning the relationship between worker self-management and economic reform are nothing new in Poland, even though their interdependence has never been perceived so clearly as now. The latter is due to the fact that the principles of economic reform currently being put into effect make explicit reference to self-management — state-owned enterprises are expected to be independent, self-managing and self-financing. But in the past, too, particularly during the years from 1956 to 1958, there have been wide-ranging and controversy-ridden discussions of self-management as part of the more comprehensive debate concerning the planning and management model to be incorporated into the national economy.[1] Although at the time there were no references to a 'self-management-orientated reform', a 'self-governing republic', or 'social enterprise', as there are at present, nevertheless worker self-management was to play an important role in the economic reforms instituted at that time. The principal demand was that decisions within the economic system be decentralised. The question thus arose as to who was to take such decentralised decisions. The endeavours to solve this dilemma led to the formulation of three conceptions of worker self-management: (a) the syndicalist conception, (b) the technocratic conception and (c) the conception of co-administration (see Hirszowicz and Morawski 1967).

---

1. Those who took part in the discussions concerning the model of socioeconomic life at that time included J. Balcerek, C. Bobrowski, B. Brus, L. Gilejko, M. Jaroszyński, S. Jędrychowski, M. Kalecki, O. Lange, E. Lipiński, B. Minc, J. Pajestka, E. Pohorille, T. Rabska, Z. Rybicki, J. Starościak and J. Wacławek.

Advocates of the syndicalist or anarcho-syndicalist conception suggested that the workers' councils which were spontaneously forming at that time should perform the most important managerial functions in the enterprise, and that a special structure above the level of workers' councils and individual state enterprises be formed, although proposals to form a special Self-government Chamber within the Seym were not usual. The assumption was that the then-existing model of planning and administration had to be radically reformed in order to prevent the resurgence of bureaucratic centralism. The best method of prevention was believed to consist of transferring management of the enterprises into the hands of a workers' council which in cooperation with the manager would ensure the independence of the enterprise. The role of the planning bodies was to be confined to the coordination and correction of plans emanating from the enterprises on the basis of market trends. While the issue of ownership was not a matter for heated discussion, it might be assumed that group ownership was a natural element in such a conception, although opinions on the issue varied.

Advocates of the technocratic conception saw in the workers' council a body of economic and technical experts who could act as advisors to the managers. In their opinion the workers' council would have to consist primarily of experts and not necessarily of blue-collar workers. They viewed the enterprise as a hierarchical and authoritarian organisation. But since they were opposed to the centralised administration of enterprises, as were the syndicalists, they recommended far-reaching decentralisation with central planning remaining intact. According to some, the experts on the council were to act as a collective management rather than acting as advisors to the managers.

Advocates of co-administration assumed that the enterprise would be run by the workers' council in conjuction with the managers. The manager would be the sole administrator of an enterprise which would be subject to central planning. Planning would be cleansed of bureaucratic deformation; for instance, the number of plan indicators imposed on the enterprise would have to be radically reduced. It was a programme of gradual decentralisation and democratisation. Decentralisation meant a greater role for the enterprise and hence also for the workers' council in the formulation of planning targets. However, the role of the council would be essentially to formulate opinions and suggest corrections — not to make decisions, since the main planning targets would remain obligatory. Democratisation was to be achieved through the performance of these functions by the workers' council on which blue-collar workers would hold no fewer than two-thirds of all seats. In this way they were expected to learn how to become the co-managers of the enterprise and how to think in terms of interests which went beyond those of their particular enterprise, thus transcending the syndicalist idea. The advocates of this conception became involved in heated controversies with the syndicalists. The idea of co-administration had the official support of the Party and the government and as such it was the version which was referred to most frequently in discussions.

None of the three conceptions was put into effect. The syndicalist version was not put into practice, because it was at variance with the theory and practice of building socialism in socialist countries; it was claimed that implementation would mean the adoption of an economy based on free competition rather than planning. Further, acceptance of the fact that workers' councils would be endowed with political power would mean that only some of the workers' interests would be represented in the decision-making process. Critics put forward the view that only a workers' party and the machinery of a state which acts in accordance with this party's recommendations could properly safeguard the interests of the working class and society as a whole.

The technocratic version was not put into effect, because, as in the previous case, it called for excessive decentralisation, and most importantly because acceptance of the technocrats' claim that the functions of management could be permanently divorced from the functions of ownership would in fact have ruled out any possibility of building socialism. This was because the idea assumed that the workers were unable to represent anything but their own narrow interests; it also assumed that control of the means of production would pass into the hands of specialist elites. This would further mean that the enterprise would be treated primarily as a technical and economic mechanism rather than a social one.

The co-administration version was not put into effect either. This was because the idea it embodied was not a coherent one. This was true both from the economic and legal point of view and the political and organisational point of view. It assumed the possibility of harmonious cooperation between a strongly centralised power apparatus which would impose ever-increasing production targets on enterprises, and the more or less democratically elected bodies which represented grass-root interests. It is my personal view that this conception, which was based on compromise, was vital from the point of view both of carrying through socialist industrialisation and the long-term interests of the working masses. The fact that a vast sphere of decision-making was left in the hands of the economic administration (i.e. the state) had to rule out the possibility of defending grass-root interests and hence precluded the development of workers' self-management. Any industrial enterprise which was increasingly divested of the ability to decide how and what to produce would inevitably have to return to carrying out tasks set by higher authorities. Thus bureaucratic centralism counteracted both the decentralisation of economic reform and industrial democracy, turning workers' self-management into an increasingly ritualistic institution which acted as a 'conveyor belt' between society and the authorities.

Under these circumstances advocates of the conservative view were able to gain the upper hand. They treated all moves towards decentralisation as a threat to the principles of a centrally planned economy and saw the possibility of the formation of a new class of socialist managers. They saw the economic experiments as being inspired by bourgeois and revisionist tendencies. They claimed that the proper conditions for the functioning of workers' councils did not yet exist, and that these councils would only add to the numbers in the bureaucratic apparatus — which in a sense turned out to be true. But their faith in the possibility of sanitising administrative mechanisms in the economy turned out to be misplaced. The number of economic parameters imposed on the enterprises went up again. Workers' self-management did not greatly stimulate industrial production and failed to defend the workers' interests (see Hirszowicz and Morawski 1967; Morawski 1973). By opposing the idea of workers' councils, advocates of this orientation proved in fact to be the allies of the rapidly expanding apparatus within the economy's administration; where decision-making was bedevilled by arbitrariness and behind-the-scenes rivalry, their interests were taken into account more frequently than those of the workers. The protection of administrative interests was accompanied by a stimulation of industrial production by the authorities and a disregard for the needs, interests and values of society as a whole; it was society who had to bear the costs of a system which was growing increasingly inefficient.

All this led to the mass rebellion which took place on December

1970. This meant that the earlier social acceptance of the goals of imposed industrialisation had gradually dissipated. This was because the economic and social experiments initiated after Gomułka's return to power in October 1956 had proved a failure. Since the mechanisms of large-scale upward social mobility, such as migration from the country to the towns, the induction of vast numbers of peasants to the working class and open access to education, no longer worked either, it seemed that the idea of co-administration could be another way of putting what people believed to be socialism into practice. However, this did not happen even though workers' councils were quite active and had involved large numbers of workers, leading to improved efficiency in the factories. From 1958 onwards, the workers' council declined in importance because the so-called Conferences of Workers' Self-management were established as the supreme authority within the self-management system. These were unwieldy and rigid bodies which apart from members of workers' councils included representatives of the Party, trade union organisations, youth organisations and so on. The tasks of these conferences were largely ritualistic in character; they confirmed the production targets imposed by the authorities but did not formulate them. Occasionally, they might amend these targets, which of course was not without significance. Under these circumstances their function of encouraging workers to implement fixed plans often dwindled to the point of non-existence.

The 'Large Economic Organisation' Reform of the 1970s

The beginning of the 1970s saw workers' protests in the coastal towns followed by similar protests in other industrial centres. However, these did not bring about any significant change to workers' self-management. This was in part a result of the nature of the demands which were raised by the workers between December 1970 and February 1971. These were primarily focused on economic issues, namely higher pay and better work conditions. The working class had had to suffer hardship for a long time: first there had been the Nazi occupation, then the reconstruction of the national economy and finally the period of forced industrialisation. The suffering and poverty which accompanied these experiences, coupled with the disappointment as to the way the economy was going, resulted in demands which were economic rather than political in nature.

But an even more important reason for the persistence of self-management in an unchanged form lay in the fact that those in power realised that economic reform would increase the productivity of the system and would be the best way of meeting the material and other needs of society. At first the authorities even mentioned comprehensive reforms, and a joint Party–government commission to work on the modernisation of the economic system was appointed. This would suggest that there was a realisation that small changes in lower-level management could not be successful if unaccompanied by changes to the entire planning and hence political system.

In the end there were no such comprehensive reforms, and proposals contained in the report submitted by the joint commission were not made widely available. Instead, the authorities decided to introduce partial reform, mainly at middle levels. Loans from the West and some economic success for the government in the early 1970s strengthened the authorities' conviction that partial reform would suffice. This reform was intended to be the beginning of a permanent process of improvement in the economic system. It concerned large economic organisations (henceforth referred to, for short, as LEO) and was implemented in 1973–6. From the economic point of view it provided for a new criterion for the evaluation of how enterprises functioned. This was the so-called additional output; salaries and wages became dependent on this criterion, which theoretically linked the earnings of workers to the performance of their enterprise. Organisationally, it modified the tripartite structure of economic administration through the creation of the LEOs. The original intention had been to replace three levels with two, but what happened was that a fourth level was added on. Socially, the reform provided for closer cooperation between the enterprises within each LEO. It did not, however, provide for the formation of self-managing bodies at the level of the LEO, with the exception of a few surrogates.

The fortunes or misfortunes of the LEO reform resembled those of the reform which was introduced in 1956. The LEO reform involved a succession of modifications to the principles behind it, resulting in an increase in the importance of administrative measures at the expense of economic measures (see Rychard 1980). That is why it was quick to crumble. The logic of an economic system whose basic elements remained unchanged led to a process whereby even those sectors of the national economy which had been included in the LEO reform gradually returned to the old practices where economic performance was based on administrative decision. It should be added that the LEO reform was to be gradually introduced into the various sectors of the economy, starting with the chemical industry.

The riots of 1976 which followed the government's decision to raise the price of foodstuffs and other goods were an indication that the Polish people were dissatisfied with both the economic and political system. For this reason another effort was made to introduce economic reforms by resorting to what was officially termed the economic manoeuvre. This involved shifting financial and material resources and manpower to the more neglected branches of the national economy. But this did not have the desired effect either. This was because the system was operating according to the old rules, or rather in the absence of any rules which might justify calling it a planning system. The system had a life of its own and soon came to dominate all of economic life. Instead of central planning, there was central administration. Promises to provide new housing and other commodities became empty phrases. The LEO reform itself became just an empty phrase, boiling down to the notion of 'perfecting the reform', implying that the economic system was already in a good state and had to be made even better. In fact, it was not in a good state and this slogan thus added to society's mistrust of the authorities.

As can be seen, the attempts to reform the national economy in the 1970s were unaccompanied by any strengthening of the processes of socialist democratisation. In this respect this period differed from the preceding one when some attempt at democratisation was made, although demands were much altered in practice. If such attempts were made in the 1970s, they were merely to serve as camouflage. In accordance with the 1978 directives of the Political Bureau, the scope of the Conferences of Workers' Self-management was extended to the entire national economy, and in 1979 there were twice as many as there had been in the preceding year. But this quantitative increase was not accompanied by any qualitative improvement. On the contrary, the general opinion is that the conferences actually deteriorated in the late 1970s. The workers' councils were in effect disbanded at that time. The Conferences of Workers' Self-management were as a rule headed by the first secretaries of the factory branches of the Party. In this way workers' self-management was formally subordinated to a political organisation which by assumption had other work to do.

At that time the authorities apparently had a certain stereotyped view of the citizen — someone who was supposed to be interested solely in his work and the acquisition of consumer goods. Under no circumstances was he expected to be a *homo politicus*. This kind of citizen seemed to be susceptible to manipulation. This philosophy differed somewhat from that espoused by Gomułka's team, who although they did not want to see the factories being run by the workers, at least accorded them a share in that process. According to Gierek's team, it was the authorities' job to govern, although they might avail themselves of the assistance of experts. The workers were there to work. If they were not willing to work or if they rebelled outright, the appropriate techniques were sought to win back their support. This could be achieved by meeting their material needs or by acting divisively and setting them against each other. But social peace could not be bought with the whole population. This was demonstrated by the events which took place in 1980 in the Lublin region and elsewhere.

The 1970s thus represented a lost opportunity. Half-hearted attempts to make changes to the national economy had ended in failure. This had many causes, among them the lack of genuine economic reform and a lack of change in the nature of industrial democracy. This led to the strike in August 1980 and to the demand for much more sweeping changes than had ever been contemplated in postwar Poland.

The Place of Worker Self-management in the Protest of 1980–1

The strikes of August 1980 resulted in renewed discussion of worker self-management and economic reform. However, from the very beginning these issues were not put forward with the vigour that they might have been. This was because the main demand of the enterprise workforces was for independent and self-governing trade unions, that is unions which would defend the interests of the employees rather than serving as a 'conveyor belt' from the authorities to the masses. The workers thus rejected what had in practice deprived them of the possibility of having their say in matters of pay, working conditions, welfare benefits and other issues which they held important. The new trade union movement, Solidarity, concentrated on consolidating the new trade unions. When the movement had gained strength, the time came for tackling questions of economic reform and worker self-management in industry.

Self-management among industrial workers was an issue over which even the leaders of the new trade unions seemed to be at odds at one point. This was because some Solidarity leaders saw a potential rival to the new unions in a system of worker self-management. The attitude of the workers themselves was a rapidly evolving one. In the late 1970s the workers and society as a whole seemed resigned to an elitist and anti-democratic social order in which there was no place for strong trade unions or strong self-government. This attitude was radically changed as a result of the strikes of August 1980. By the spring and autumn of 1981 there was a widely held belief that enterprise self-management was vital, although opinions were still divided as to the urgency of the issue.[2] The debate generated by the planned economic reform outlined in a report published by a governmental commission on economic reform accelerated the formulation of the opinion voiced both by Solidarity leaders and the workers themselves, that a new kind of worker self-management was imperative. It was thought that the expected economic reform could only bring a breakthrough if the workers were directly committed to carrying it out. Many of those contributing to the debate thought in the light of their experiences in the aftermath of 1956 that the version of worker self-management put forward in the government's plan must by definition be a limited one, even though self-management was one of the three pillars of the planned reform. The other two fundamental elements of the plan, the autonomy and self-financing of enterprises, aroused similar doubts.

Another important argument was added to the debate when Solidarity concluded that it should concentrate on the protection of workers' rights. Could decisions relating to production and the economy be left to the economic administration? It was argued that if this was what happened, the chances of genuine economic reform would be minimal. If reform was left to the state authorities and the administrative machinery of the economy, it would be either bu-

---

2. See the communiqué on the public opinion survey carried out after the first part of the Solidarity Congress and published by the Centre for the Study of Public Opinion at Polish Radio and Television in September 1981. See also the communiqué on the worker self-management questionnaire published by the Centre for Social Studies at Solidarity's Mazovian Branch.

reaucratic or technocratic, which in the light of previous experience would mean that it would end in failure. But if reform were to be influenced by social pressure, and above all under pressure from Solidarity, it had a chance of becoming political reform. As one journalist wrote at the time: 'Anyone with any knowledge of economics and able to draw conclusions will see that economic reform without political reform is impossible. Moreover, if econ-omic reform is successfully implemented it will result in an evol-ution of political structures, in the abandonment of the bureaucratic centralist model of socialism in the economy and outside it' (Surdy-kowski, n.d.).

In tune with many others, this author demanded that Solidarity should not confine itself to the supervision of the government, for this would be the death-knell of reform. Rather, Solidarity should be a responsible co-instigator of reform. In practice this meant the support of worker self-management. This view gained ground as Solidarity was transformed into a social movement willing to as-sume responsibility for the shaping of a new socio-political order. In this order both economic reform and worker self-management were to play key roles. In the summer of 1981 these two elements became closely intertwined; the period saw the emergence of a conception of reform and self-management which was in compe-tition with the one previously put forward by the government. This conception was a product of the grass-root movement which was in favour of comprehensive, radical and democratic economic reform. 'The socialisation of what has been nationalised' was the watchword in the debates. This explicit formulation did not occur until the summer of 1981, that is about one year after the strikes of August 1980.

Worker Self-management in Governmental and Non-governmental Planned Economic Reform

In 1981 there were many proposals as to how worker self-management was to fit into the economic system, and in particular how it would link with economic reform. Often these proposals embodied very different ideas of worker self-management and economic reform. Discussion most frequently centred on the government plan which had been published in January and the plan advocated by Solidarity and known as the Network Plan, after a group of seventeen Solidarity enterprise representatives. The Network Plan was published in July 1981 as the non-government draft of the State Enterprise Act.[3] While the plans had many important points in common, there were also many differences due, I believe, to the different organisational principles embodied in the respective plans. I would like to underline these essential differences by analysing the two sets of proposals and other comments which were made on the subject at that time.[4]

All parties were agreed as to the necessity of organising a genuine system of worker self-management, but could not agree as to where it should come in the hierarchy of authority.

The Autonomy of Enterprises

In the draft of the government's Act, the safeguarding of the public interest in the day-to-day operation of the enterprises was to be achieved, on the one hand, through the use of the economic instruments in the hands of the state, such as the tax and credit systems, customs and excise, the central fixing of prices, contracts between the state and specific enterprises (e.g. for military production), and it was to such measures that the non-government proposals were exclusively confined. On the other hand, government proposals also made reference to such imprecisely defined mechanisms as 'information measures', 'administrative measures', 'legal provisions', 'the allocation of specific tasks', 'the appointment of managers', 'supervision by state authorities' and various other forms of supervision and assessment of enterprises. This shows that those who had drawn up the government proposals were apprehensive of situations where indirect economic measures would be inadequate to protect the public interest; an effort had been made to provide the central authorities with additional means whereby they could exercise influence on the enterprises. By way of contrast, the non-government proposals viewed such a solution not only as a threat to the autonomy of the enterprise and the interests of the employees, but as a threat to the public interest as well.

3. See *Przeglåd Techniczny*, January 1981, and *Życie i Nowoczesność* (the *Życie Warszawy* supplement), 9 July 1981.
4. Participants in the discussion included S. Albinowski, J. Beksiak, L. Bar, W. Baka, A. Bocheński, C. Bobrowski, K. Doktór, S. Jakubowicz, T. Jaworski, C. Józefiak, J. Gościński, J. Kaleta, R. Krawczyk, T. Kowalik, K. Kloc, W. Kuczyński, A.K. Kozmiński, A. Łopatka, B. Minc, J. Pajestka, R. Pluta, J. Pietrucha, J. Strzelecki, S. Włodyka and A. Zawiślak.

The authors of the non-government proposals thought that the government proposals merely involved a decentralisation of managerial decisions, although it was admitted that the decentralisation was more sweeping than anything which had been experienced in the socialist countries until then. However, the enterprises were to remain directly subordinate to the central authorities. The non-government proposals had something more in view than mere decentralisation. They called for a shift of authority within the economy from the state administration to enterprise employees and their representatives. It must be added that these proposals did not urge the abolition of central planning but envisaged changes in the way such planning might be realised in practice.

The proposals were interpreted as involving the authorities within the economy becoming independent of the political authorities; the authors of the proposals willingly accepted this interpretation. In my view a better way of putting it would be to say that the proposals sought to change the way political authority was exercised within the economy; the enterprises were no longer to be administratively subordinate to the political authorities. It was not intended to introduce anarchy into the economy, nor to cause the economy to revert to a free-competition stage of capitalism, though such voices were also raised. The intention, rather, was to transform the way in which decisions were transmitted from the authorities at the top to the enterprises.

The Manager and Self-management

The government proposals saw the manager as the administrative agent of the enterprise. But in representing enterprise staff, worker self-management also had 'the right and duty to participate in management' and thus could make the manager the executor of its decisions. Thus in a sense these were two equal parties endowed with different prerogatives. It was assumed that they would supervise one another, because a provision was included allowing either party to block a decision made by the other. In contrast with this, the non-government proposals assumed that the workers' self-managing body would make managerial decisions which would have to be put into effect by the manager; that is, the manager would be subordinate to this body. Related to this were the different suggestions put forward concerning how the manager was to be appointed. In the government proposals the most frequent view was that he should be appointed by the authorities, while the non-government proposals saw the manager as an appointee of the workers' self-management body. According to the government proposals, the manager would be accountable to a lesser extent to the workers' self-management and to a greater extent to the higher administrative authorities; this would make him the representative of the state in the enterprise. The non-government proposals saw the manager as being accountable solely to the workers' self-management.

In other words, the government proposals put forward the idea of co-management, with the participation of worker self-management in the management of the enterprise. In this they made reference to Article 13 of the Polish Constitution, which states that workers are entitled to participate in the management of the enterprise. The non-government proposals, on the other hand, wanted to see self-management taking managerial decisions which would have been in accordance with Articles 5 and 11 of the Constitution, which state that social property is to be consolidated and that the socialist economic system is based on the socialised means of production.

It might be added that the government proposals referred to solutions put forward in 1956 which provided for the participation of workers' councils in management; the non-government proposals seemed to have come to the conclusion that the workers' councils had proved a failure because they had not had sufficient power.

The Controversy over Forms of Property

The government proposals talked about state-owned enterprises while the non-government proposals referred to social enterprises. This was not simply a verbal quibble, although that might sometimes have seemed to be the case. State property implies management by the state, while social property implies management by society. The critics of the non-government proposals thought that the abandonment of the state property clause meant the substitution of public property with group property since the employees of an enterprise were to have exclusive rights over the property of the enterprise and the enterprise was to be run by the workers' self-management. After certain amendments, the non-government proposals formulated the issue as follows: 'The enterprise has rights over that part of public property which has been entrusted to it by "the founding agency" [i.e. the authorities — Ed. (M.W.)]; that is to say, the means of production are not owned by the workers but by society at large, and the founding agency merely entrusts them on behalf of the state to the enterprise where the latter is a legal person'. This formulation comes close to those found in the government proposals.

The controversy over the nature of ownership was clearly summed up by Piotrowska-Hochfeld (1982):

> Self-management in the sphere of production has also been criticised at the political and doctrinal level. The advocates of the government's solutions feared that state property as such would vanish, becoming transformed into group property. This misunderstanding was based on the identification of ownership with management. Owners may cede their right to manage their property to a group of persons who do not thereby become the owners of the property they manage. This was exactly the situation in the case of the state-owned enterprises which managed that part of the national property which was assigned to them. The problem thus was not the imaginary danger that group property or ownership would be reinstated, but whether a designated part of the national property would be run by workers' self-management or by the state administration, and the relations which should exist between owner and manager.

One Legislative Act or Two?

From the outset the government proposals envisaged the drawing up of two separate legal Acts, one dealing with the enterprise and the other with worker self-management. The non-government proposals called for a single legislative Act since the passing of two separate Acts might have suggested that the institution of worker self-management was not an integral part of the functioning of the enterprise. This apprehension could have been due to past experience where successive Acts and/or enactments concerned with worker self-management were not treated as binding by the administrators of the economy. Those who advocated the idea of two separate legislative Acts were of the opinion that economic reform meant that many Acts dealing with economic issues would have to be passed. In addition to the State Enterprises Act and the Worker Self-management Act, there would have to be other Acts dealing with various issues concerning the enterprises; it would therefore be impossible to deal with all these issues in a single Act.

These controversies were not the only ones to emerge during the debate taking place in 1980–1, but for the moment we shall confine ourselves to them. They reached a peak the day before the Seym passed both the State Enterprises Act and the State Enterprise Worker Self-management Act on 25 September 1981. The texts of both Acts were based on a compromise reached by the two parties, and the solutions they embodied were as follows:

Ad A. The autonomy of the enterprise was explicitly stressed in the formulation 'state agencies can make decisions relating to a state enterprise only in cases provided for by legislative Acts' (Art. 4.2 of the State Enterprises Act). It was stressed that the enterprise functions on the basis of its own plan and that the compliance of that plan with the targets envisaged in the national plan would be defined in separate legislative acts dealing with planning, statistical reports, financing, taxation, the formation and use of special funds and price-fixing. Furthermore, Article 54 of the same Act stated that 'the founding agency is entitled to impose upon a state enterprise the duty to include special tasks in its plan and to assign to an enterprise tasks not included in its plan if the demands made by national defence, natural disasters and the fulfilment of international obligations required it'.

It has to be said that as far as the protection of the autonomy of state enterprises and worker self-management was concerned, the formulations embodied in the Acts were a big step forward relative to the legal regulations in force prior to 25 September 1981. Self-management gained independence from political and trade union organisations, and this was in marked contrast with the proposed function of the Workers' Self-management Conference put forward in the preceding period.

Ad B. The dilemma as to whether the self-managing body was to play a role in management or to manage the enterprise itself was resolved so that the enterprise authorities would include both the manager and the general meeting of the employees or their delegates, and the workers' council. But the State Enterprises Act reads '[the manager] administers the enterprise and is its external representative'. Further, the Self-management Act states that 'the employees participate in the management of the enterprise' and the manager 'carries out the decisions of the workers' council'. Taken together, the meaning of these two formulations is somewhat obscure, especially since it is not stated precisely which agency has binding prerogatives in which matters. But it must be said that many of the most important prerogatives of the self-managing body are explicitly listed.

The manager is appointed and dismissed by the founding agency or by the workers' council. The founding agency only does this (a) if a given enterprise is on the list of enterprises of central importance to the national economy which is drawn up by the cabinet in cooperation with the trade unions or (b) if it is of public utility. Thus it is only the list of enterprises of fundamental importance to the economy which may be a matter of possible controversy.

Ad C. As far as the issue of ownership is concerned, enterprises are termed 'state enterprises', which precludes the possibility of interpreting the Act to refer to enterprises as group property.

Ad D. The Seym passed two Acts, one dealing with enterprises and the other dealing with worker self-management.

The Reforms and Self-management: The Pros and Cons

During the years from 1956 to 1980, the debate surrounding worker self-management was expressed in terms of centralisation versus decentralisation. Decentralised functions were to be performed by the self-managing body alone or in conjunction with the manager of the enterprise; in practice, the latter was usually the case. The terms of the debate changed in 1980–1, when at least some parties in the discussions took the institution of self-management to be the central pillar of economic reform and the starting point for any debate related to this reform. According to some, it was not the system of planning and management which determined the functions of self-management; on the contrary, self-management was held to define the necessary changes in the system of planning and management (see Szwarc 1981). Thus reform was to be self-management orientated.

The arguments advanced in favour of this solution were general rather than pragmatic. It was often stated that reform was bound to fail if the old institutions and mechanisms were preserved. It was bound to fail because it would be based on the idea that the form of socialism with which the Poles are familiar (i.e. nationalisation) represents the essence of socialism instead of being a transitory historical phase on the path to true socialisation. Socialism's current form has many serious defects — for example, centralised decision-making, the dominance of the administrative machinery, lobbying and tug-of-war behind the scenes, the central imposition of production targets and allocation of funds, the lack of separation between political and economic power, the role of the state as the sole entrepreneur and employer, which is conducive to excessive bureaucracy and inimical to any form of non-government supervision, and so on.

The advocates of radical economic reform claimed that only a system based on self-management would work because only this kind of system could guarantee a better way of dealing with property; that is to say, it would guarantee the socialisation of property. The previous forms of socialising relations in industry — the participation of workers in the work of voluntary organisations, the co-management of workers' councils and trade union activity — were not capable of ensuring this (see Pańków 1981b). All this of course meant depriving the administrative apparatus of its exclusive right to control the national economy. This was exactly the point in question; so much distrust of the apparatus had accumulated that no reform which it carried out would ever be able to gain credibility. In short, it was not possible to resort to managerial reform of the type which had been introduced earlier in Hungary.

The advocates of reform based on self-management also emphasised the importance of pragmatic considerations. They expected that a self-management system would encourage greater interest on the part of workers in the productivity of their enterprise, since profits would be shared not only by managerial elites but by all the workers. On a broader scale, this would mean building the principle of negotiations and social contracts into the economic system, principles which had previously been non-existent in practice. In most cases, however, the methods whereby self-management were to give workers an interest in productivity and economic factors in general were not specified. Nor was it said what the negotiation system in self-management was to be like. The latter does not apply to suggestions that a self-management chamber be organised within the Seym. It must be borne in mind that the discussions were primarily concerned with the level of the enterprise, at least during the first stage. However, even at this level people failed to foresee that conflicts between the self-management body and the trade unions would emerge.

The advocates of self-management-based reforms were of the opinion that genuine worker self-management would prove even more important than the autonomous and self-governing trade unions. This was because the latter could be reconciled with a centralist or even a capitalist system. In other words, the advocates of radical economic reform based on self-management thought that only through taking power within the enterprise would it be possible to carry out radical economic reform and get the country out of the crisis. They did not follow this through with an analysis of the consequences involved in the substitution of one form of political domination by another, that is from state-based domination to self-management-based domination.

Many different arguments were raised against these radical views, but only a few were targeted against self-management as such. In most cases the arguments against a radical interpretation of the role of self-government included recommendations that reform be linked to the introduction of proper economic mechanisms and the adoption of an effective system for the dismissal or replacement of those managers hostile to reform.

More frequent were views which stressed the idea of worker self-management itself without attaching very great expectations to it. Those expressing this view thought that over-confidence in self-regulatory mechanisms, a common characteristic of the advocates of radical self-management-orientated reforms, resulted from a disregard of the economic realities. Mieszczankowski, who formulated a down-to-earth criticism of the government commission proposals, blamed the commission for spreading such views (see Jermakowicz 1981). According to him, competition was not possible when combined with a form of social ownership and market shortages. On the other hand, competition *de facto* eliminated central planning, which was necessary because decisions had to be transmitted downwards from the central authorities. The system suggested by the commission was to have been based on self-regulation without self-regulatory mechanisms. As Mieszczankowski put it, this would result in a national economy which would be neither planned nor market-based, but rather anarchy-based. Mieszczankowski also observed certain advantages in the proposals he was criticising, but thought that they would only be felt after 1990.

In the eyes of yet other participants in the debate, worker self-management was not so much an integral element of economic reform as a social movement which could play an important role in economic reform if other elements such as the state administration, the Party and the trade unions failed. They had in mind the pressure which worker self-management could exert on the economy's administration to induce the latter to give reform the right shape. According to this idea, self-management could assist in achieving the reform of fundamental economic mechanisms. The institution of self-management would act as a political shield for reform rather than as an important element in its own right within the enterprise.

The solution ultimately adopted by the Seym differed from those outlined above. It was not as radical as the non-government proposals, nor as minimalistic as those mentioned above, where the acceptance of self-management was seen as a tactical consideration and not as a central issue in systemic reform. In fact, it represented a kind of compromise. Not only did it take into account the opinions presented above, it also gave room to the type of thinking extremely common in economic practice, especially after the introduction of martial law, with the resulting suspension of the activities of the existing worker self-management bodies. This thinking assumed that in an economic crisis worker self-management could be a drawback because it might hinder the taking of operational decisions by the administration. It is common knowledge that a substantial section of managers has always been against self-management or in favour of that version embodied by the Conferences of Worker Self-management. The reasons for the latter are obvious: under certain circumstances this kind of self-management could help managers manipulate both the higher authorities and the workers.

Thus the solution adopted represented a compromise based on three standpoints. Firstly, the radical conception of reform contributed the idea of making worker self-management one of the pillars of economic reform; this led to the slogan-like description of the enterprise as autonomous, self-managing and self-financing. But self-management did not become the main element of reform or the universal solution. The self-government formula was to be applied to a wide section of enterprises, but others were to be more 'state-dependent', which meant that in such cases self-management rights would be more limited. Secondly, the minimalistic views contributed the idea of making self-management one of the driving forces of reform, but the other two elements were no less important. The economic system was to be based on autonomous and self-financing enterprises. The third approach, which treated self-management formalistically and as an instrument of manipulation, contributed nothing in formal terms to the final solution. However, in practical terms it might be expected that the preservation of the strategic role of the central plan and such administrative entities as the ministries and associations of enterprises, together with the hope that the central political system could work better, ensured the decisive role of the authorities at the top; the managers were used to this role and could not imagine a socialist economy without it. Thus worker self-management could not be fully autonomous; there is nothing wrong with this in itself, for one can hardly imagine a modern national economy, especially in a socialist state, which is deprived of the possibility of central control, However, the point is that there is more than one way in which the central authorities can control enterprises; in the case of small-scale purely cosmetic modifications of the system of centralised control, all changes within the enterprises are doomed to failure.

Why Is Worker Self-management Indispensable?

I shall now examine worker self-management and economic reform from the point of view of the satisfaction of worker interests. This is important because both the crisis of 1980–1 and the earlier crises have shown that behind-the-scenes lobbying and tug-of-war caused some of the major dysfunctions of the economic system. This tug-of-war was due to the assumption that there was an insuperable conflict between the enterprise and society at large, and that this conflict could only be resolved by the state instituting specific mechanisms to reconcile these and other interests. This was supported by the belief that only the state was in a position to ensure that general interests prevailed over particular, short-term ones.

However, a glance at the Polish experience since 1945 is enough to contradict this optimistic view. The successive crises have demonstrated that the political and administrative decision-making structures can easily be dominated by various particular interests (e.g. those of specific industries), and that this can be detrimental to the interests of large social groups and society as a whole. Consolidation of particular interests merely exacerbates the structural imbalances in the national economy so that what had been a policy (e.g. the expansion of heavy industry and certain other specialised industries), gradually becomes a denial of all policy and a show of strength on the part of the industry representatives.

99

Crisis and Transition

It might be said that this has been the result of the programme of industrialisation and associated organisation of production adopted by the central authorities which was bound to impose certain long-term burdens on society. However, the point is that such burdens can be distributed in different ways. Until the mid-1960s there was some apparent approval on the part of Polish society for the industrialisation policy. In it, it seemed to see the satisfaction of social aspirations, namely the opportunity for upward social mobility in its various forms and on a mass scale: migration from country to town, achievement of the status of manual or white-collar workers, opportunities for a better education for oneself and one's children, and so on. The net effect was that state ownership and state control in the running of the various areas of socioeconomic life in Poland did not raise major objections. But from the mid-1960s onwards the efficiency of the system decreased perceptibly, which led to progressive and regular outbursts of social protest.

Previously, endeavours to extirpate the evil invariably followed the same course, namely an increase in the autonomy of the economic sphere. Economic reforms, or rather attempted reforms since they were always half-hearted and usually unsuccessful, can now be seen as involving a change in the rules whereby targets were transmitted by the political system to the economic system and society. The trend of such changes was always the same: the increased influence of the national economy and society at large upon politics. In no case, however, was a harmonious relationship between these two systems achieved. After some time elapsed, the political system would once more begin to dominate the economy, initially to the detriment of the latter, but later to the detriment of both, and society as a whole.

It must be said that before 1980 there was never any attempt to reverse the political determination of the economy; instead there was an attempt to make this influence indirect rather than direct in form. This entailed the decentralisation of decision-making and the according of certain rights to worker self-management. However, the fundamental characteristics of the system remained unchanged. The events of 1980–1 represented an attempt to reverse the direction of determination; society and the requirements of the national economy were to determine the functioning of the political system. In time this led to a paralysis of the state. The halting of this process through the introduction of martial law in December 1981 does not remove the problem as to whether the structure of the state in the narrow sense of the term is capable of being modified so as to be able to meet social interests voiced at grass-roots level. Without this the country would sooner or later experience new protests. The issue is how these deprived interests can be permanently included in the decision-making structure of the state.

One possible solution would be for all group interests to have genuine political representation. This could assume different forms according to the level at which a given group functions. In creating the conception of what was termed the self-governing republic, attention was focused on the lowest levels. This created the impression that the political system would be a loose federation of autonomous self-governing systems or sub-systems, which would not be too well integrated by the political mechanisms superimposed upon it. We would thus be dealing with an enormously expanded pluralism in political life where there would be no concern for the interests of the whole.

The idea that there was a need to provide for genuine political representation at higher levels was also expressed. Here I am referring to the suggestions for the adoption a political institution in the form of a second chamber in the Seym, which would be referred to as the Chamber of Self-government or the Chamber of Labour, which would have in view the interests of society as a whole. This would mean, however, that the autonomy of worker self-management in individual enterprises would be reduced since the enterprises would have to take into account the needs of the national economy and the state.

There was also an intermediate option which assumed a *sui generis* division of labour in the form of a hierarchical structuring of decision-making. In practice this would have meant that some strategic decisions would be made at the top while others might be made at enterprise level, for example. How rights would be distributed would depend on a number of factors, some technical, some organisational and some socio-political in character.

In general terms it may be stated that while the emergence of the new trade unions favoured the raising of the issue of political representation, no discussion of the organisational framework of the political system in Poland developed. In all probability this would have taken place before elections to the Seym and the people's councils.

A second possible solution would have involved the formation of various consultative and opinion-making bodies such as a consultative economic council attached to the government or a socioeconomic council attached to the Seym. These would not function as institutions of political representation but could contribute to the decision-making process. This was merely a possibility and it is debatable whether social interests could be genuinely represented in this way since the basic decision-making structure would be unchanged. However, these proposals reveal a genuine intention to make these structures more effective.

A third possible solution was based on the optimistic view that administrative and economic bureaucracy is capable of learning. However, the bureaucracy is very limited in this regard. Only changes initiated in a flexible and innovation-orientated political system — that is, one which ensures the proper representation of all social interests — is capable of forcing bureaucracy to change. Otherwise such change can only be apparent, not real.

Let us now turn to the relationship between the various conceptions of economic reform and the three possible solutions listed here. Let us begin with the third solution, which assumes that it is possible for bureaucratic structures to be somehow cleansed. From a radical view of self-management-orientated economic reform, these structures would have to be destroyed since they are incapable of change. From the point of view of the minimalistic proposals the structures would have to be weakened since they would always be opposed to far-reaching reform. Finally, from the official point of view, their performance would have to be improved, and they would have to be complemented by a structure based on self-management.

The second possibility, that of instituting consultative and opinion-giving bodies was in 1980–1 seen as being defective in view of the failure of expert opinion during the 1970s. The idea was given more credence in 1982–3.

The first possibility, which was the most sweeping of the proposed forms of economic reform, envisaged the political representation of those interests which had until then been more or less ignored. It was only mentioned in connection with the debate on the place of the trade unions in Polish public life and in connection with the issue of the second chamber in the Seym. The problem was bound to emerge before the elections to the Seym. Obviously, the role which Solidarity started to play was related to this issue — from the conclusion of an agreement with the government authorities in 1980 to its numerous negotiations with the government, to the transformation of the union into a social movement before it was suspended with the proclamation of martial law. But from the very outset Solidarity's approach was marked by a specific one-sidedness inasmuch as it formulated demands without assuming any responsibility whatever for the consequences. It was only when Solidarity started to promote the idea of self-management that it also started to think differently and began to assume responsibility in economic matters. However, as has been said, until December 1981 Solidarity's proposals were almost exclusively confined to the level of the enterprise and did not refer to the political and economic system as a whole.

Another feature of the 1980–1 discussions deserves attention. There was a tendency to seek the best, the single perfect solution with the wholesale rejection of all other possibilities. This meant that solutions which had been effective in the past were also dismissed. In my own opinion a better strategy would have been to complement existing structures with new ones where the old ones were defective. Thus the mechanisms of the Polish economy should also have structures based on self-management, particularly if these have proved more effective than state structures. However, I do not hold that such new structures should invariably and by definition be accorded priority. Self-managing enterprises do not inevitably function better than others. In Western economies they often lose out in competition with other firms, although it must be stressed that they have proved themselves in some industries. On the whole, however, they are somewhat less efficient than the best capitalist firms. When it comes to the socialist countries, the only example we have is Yugoslavia; elsewhere there are no enterprises based on self-management. When we take foreign experience as a whole into account we can see that under Polish conditions self-managed enterprises might be an interesting experiment, one to be recommended, particularly in view of the low level of efficiency in state-run enterprises.

Rejection of the existing system, however, need not lead to the conclusion that self-managing enterprises are a panacea for the crisis in the Polish national economy and for the inefficiency of Polish enterprises. Yet criticism of the system has led to the recommendation of things which were new but untested. Structures based on self-management should be weighed up against the advantages of other solutions, including the bureaucratic solution where simple and repetitive tasks are involved. If they are not, we will end up with the substitution of one form of political control of the enterprise with another which will not necessarily be better.

Under Polish conditions a self-managing enterprise could become an alternative for those bureaucratic solutions which are quite evidently ineffective. In view of the total mistrust of the solutions advocated by the central authorities, this would have the not insignificant merit of being formulated at grass-roots level and thus having a chance of being socially approved. This is even more important when one considers that the Polish Treasury does not have the means of ensuring the high level of consumption which could help the authorities to win social acceptance for their policies. Self-managing enterprises thus seem to be a way of safeguarding worker interests in a period of economic reform and economic crisis. This solution carries with it many unknowns, but the risk involved in managerial reform is no smaller. The latter would be deeply mistrusted by society and the failure of similar attempts in the past would be remembered.

Alternative Solutions

So far we have been contrasting the merits of a bureaucratic solution as opposed to one based on self-management. But these are not the only two options available. The bureaucratic system is the one we know best. It has been part of the construction of the socialist system and is becoming increasingly inefficient. All attempts at economic reform, two of them major, have ended in failure. This is what has led to the economic crisis in Poland. If the present system of management and decision-making persists, then even if the present crisis comes to an end, there is no guarantee that another will not occur. On the contrary, it is almost bound to happen.

In my view the fundamental cause of the inefficiency of the system lies in the fact that activating mechanisms instigated by the central authorities take precedence over mechanisms whereby social interests may be articulated at grass-roots level. This is why the interests of society and the values it espouses are not sufficiently taken into account in the political and economic system. Socialist democratic institutions such as trade unions and worker self-management acted as a kind of 'conveyor-belt' for the transmission of instructions downwards rather than as the representative of grass-roots interests. This made the system, which was already highly centralised, even more bureaucratic.

Added to this was the fact that political solutions were borrowed from an entirely different economic, political and cultural environment, where there had been some justification for them. Thus the coercive elements of policy acquired such dimensions that they discredited the system in the eyes of society. The declining efficiency of the economic system combined with the lack of universal acceptance of the political system accounts for the fact that we are now witnessing the rejection of that version of socialism which we have experienced and which we term 'bureaucratic socialism'. However, the ideals behind the system have not been rejected, nor has socialism in general.

The alternative to the bureaucratic system is now a system based on self-management. Proposals for a self-management-orientated system evolved from dissatisfaction with the bureaucratic system and included the feature which that system lacked. The proposals were mainly concerned with theoretical ideas, and this is probably why they contained so many utopian elements; much less attention was paid to the harsh realities of economic life. However, notions relating to a self-management system were maturing and becoming more realistic; it is difficult to say what their final form might have been.

In contrast to the bureaucratic system which is constructed from the top downwards, the self-management system was the product of a spontaneous grass-roots movement which was trying to find its own solutions. The movement was exceedingly sensitive to external manipulation and exaggerated the radical aspects of its ideas. This militated against their implementation. The movement had few supporters in the power elite since its arguments were largely targeted against it. On this score it differed from the self-management system in Yugoslavia, which had been the creation of the Party and which both Party and society were working to improve.

The self-management system was intended to be the opposite of the bureaucratic system, and since the latter was the only form of socialism which had been experienced, the self-management system was sometimes thought of as being anti-socialist. However, some of its advocates termed the system 'self-management-based socialism', and this was in fact the programme formulated in many non-government proposals concerning the enterprise, the national economy and society in general. On the whole, these programmes did not make any reference to capitalist models. They rather assumed that in a modern democratic society not everything can be organised through the state machinery and that was why structures based on self-management deserved support.

The third possibility was that of a technocratic system which laid stress on a professional approach to problems. This was to be reflected in institutional solutions which should embody a consistent approach to change in the existing system with a view to systemic reform, for example. This reform could become the watchword of the system, just as industrialisation was the watchword for a bureaucratic system which was subordinate to the political authorities for whom industrialisation was the means to a revolutionary end. Consistent reform therefore requires not conformists but experts. The system would rely on engineers, technologists, economists and other specialists. Ideology played no leading role; it was treated as an instrument of manipulation, not an object of faith.

The construction of a technocratic system requires a political decision — that much is beyond doubt. But would it be possible to carry through technocratic reform in Poland where self-governing bodies would play only a consultative role? Were such reform to succeed, it would rid the country of the many uncertainties associated with the self-management system. This, in my view, was the central dilemma of the period immediately after Gierek's rise to power in December 1970. The answer, I think, is relatively simple. The technocratic system must be rejected, and this for several reasons. It would intensify society's mistrust of the authorities; it would fail to release the energy concentrated in large social groups; it could have unexpected and undesirable economic consequences for people whose living standards have already fallen, and it could arouse the resistance of the conservative power apparatus, which would have to be removed because of their lack of competence. The opportunity for this kind of reform did in my view exist in the early 1970s but the political rulers at the time did not take advantage of it.

It appears that the only option left is the development of democratic institutions. It is easier to characterise the institutional features of this kind of system in negative rather than positive terms. The first condition for the construction of the new system would be the rejection of the patterns of bureaucratic socialism. Patterns of socialism based on self-management should be tested gradually since there is no doubt that economic management exercised by the state administration has many failings and should be abolished. But reliance on self-governing bodies should not lead to an excessive pluralisation of social life, with all the threat of anarchy that this entails. Modern industrial society, including socialist society, must have a strong centre which takes political and economic decisions with the long-term needs of society and the national economy in mind. This centre must derive its strength from society's acceptance of it, and this in turn means that there must be institutions to represent grass-roots interests. These should be hierarchical; that is, they should be formed at the base but also be represented at a national level.

Recent Experience

The reader might infer from what has been said so far that Poland's socioeconomic life has been dominated by controversies over ideas, or that events are crucially shaped by these controversies. This would be an erroneous impression. In the post-1945 period, doctrine played a significant role in the formation of the Polish economic system, but in recent years its importance has dwindled considerably. Recent events in the economy have rather been a result of the impact of various social forces whose influence has changed over time. It is not the attainment of goals formulated in discussions which strikes one, as much as the fluctuation of a situation which is more or less determined by social forces representing specific interests, the satisfaction of which often takes the form of ideological demands.

The fate of economic reform and worker self-management exemplify the fluidity of Polish social life and the way in which different forces are exerted on it. Prior to the imposition of martial law, self-management existed in roughly 50 per cent of enterprises. These bodies were modelled along various lines, but usually bore most resemblance to what had been put forward in the non-government proposals.[5] They did not have an opportunity to consolidate before they were suspended with the introduction of martial law. Yet soon afterwards the authorities decided that their activities might be restored on application by the manager to the

5. See 'Szanse przeszczepu' (The transplantation's chances), an interview with Professor Janusz Gościński by Jerzy Szperkowickz, in *Przegląd Techniczny*, 1981, no. 19.

minister or voivodeship governor concerned. However, there were very few such applications during the initial period, and in even fewer cases was permission granted.

Many aspects of economic reform were deliberately suspended in the face of the deepening economic crisis. Not only was self-management abolished, but there was an introduction of so-called operational programmes and controlled prices, the appointment of government representatives to carry out specific tasks and the obligatory association of enterprises. According to some observers, all this modified the nature of reform; according to others, it nipped it in the bud.

These facts allow us to conclude that economic reform and worker self-management in the form put forward in 1981 are now seriously threatened. What was then universal acceptance of reform and expanding worker self-management has proved to be only a *sui generis* tactical alliance, and few social groups are still interested in them. Various surveys have shown that many managers are against self-management, preferring production targets and the distribution of funds and resources to be set by the authorities since this relieves them of responsibility for decisions. It has been emphasised that workers are not very interested in self-management either, although the surveys do show them to be more interested than the managers. The public reaction to economic reform is vague because in the public mind reform is associated with high prices, food rationing and other unpleasant conditions which are rather a consequence of the parlous state of the Polish economy than of economic reform *per se*.

The fact remains that all this is conducive to the revival of the old organisational structures and the persistence of tug-of-war mechanisms. This is observable in the relationship between the enterprises and the banks, where the latter yield to pressure and allow 'soft financing'. This in turn raises the question as to whether the reform has exceeded its own 'critical mass', for its advocates consider this to be a *sine qua non* of radical reform. It is claimed that the present crisis is a result not so much of a system based on the imposition of production targets and the allotment of funds and resources, a system which works well in the German Democratic Republic and Czechoslovakia, as much as of a series of misguided economic and political decisions taken by Gierek and his team. It should be emphasised that this an infrequently expressed view. The prevalent thinking assumes the need for economic reform as a gradually accelerating process as economic stability is attained.

In my opinion the latter approach is too cautious and does not guarantee that the economic crisis will be dealt with quickly or that economic reform will be carried out. On the contrary, it might prolong the crisis and bury reform. Reform would then become a myth. For some, the expectations associated with reform would be excessive, looking for positive changes in too many spheres of social and economic life. For others it would merely be an indication that changes in the national economy are necessary, and if they were initiated, this would be regarded as the achievement of reform regardless of what had really been attained.

Concluding Remarks

Economic reform is necessary if Poland is to develop socioeconomically, if there is to be a rise in living standards and if socio-cultural aspirations are to be satisfied. The economic system has to its credit the transformation of Poland from a predominantly agricultural country into a modern industrial state. But the system has ceased to be efficient. The same applies to economic development strategy, which has been questioned since the 1960s in a cycle of social conflict. This conflict arose because the economy was not being run properly; the system did not take the growing complexity of an industrial society into account. From the sociological point of view, there was no room for the expression of social values and interests in a system which was orientated above all towards the rapid socioeconomic mobilisation of society.

The events which took place in Poland in August 1980 marked a turning-point in attempts to construct a grass-roots system for the articulation of interests and values. Following the protests of 1956 and 1970, the Poles had confidence in the authorities' attempts to improve social and economic conditions. However, the general opinion in 1980–1 was that it was society itself which should undertake these changes; the authorities had lost credibility. The conflict between the authorities on the one hand and society on the other had become the principal social issue.

Worker self-management and economic reform were merely two of many reforms formulated in 1980–1. They are not new, but since after the promise of reform, economic life has repeatedly reverted to its old patterns in the past; it is feared that the authorities plan the same thing this time. The authorities themselves are in an uneviable situation since it is their task to turn slogans into fact in a situation of grave economic crisis.

In their endeavour to turn slogans into reality, the authorities encounter numerous obstacles, including ideological ones. For example, they have tried to eliminate social conflict whereas this conflict is a normal part of the functioning of a complex industrial society. The only possible solution is to regulate this conflict by establishing institutions which can articulate social values and interests. Clashes of interest can be the driving force of progress, as Marxist social theory has shown. In addition to autonomous and self-governing trade unions, worker self-management could act as one such institution.

The economic obstacles are also formidable, while obstacles of a social nature are no less difficult to overcome. A powerful bureaucracy in administration and in the economy has emerged. It has its own interests and values and is to a large extent independent of both the supreme political authorities to which it is linked, and of society. On the other hand, society has developed a passivity and wait-and-see attitude which is not always conducive to efficient work. That is why it is hard for the slogan and principle of economic reform to permeate society; only an innovation-orientated society can rapidly assimilate the principles of reform. For this reason it is important that the image of the authorities held by society should improve; without this improvement all reform initiated by the authorities is eyed with suspicion.

Finally, there are the political obstacles. Political reform is a *sine qua non* of economic reform. However, for some individuals within the establishment this means loss of power; that is why they are opposed to all reform, both political and economic. The more far-sighted within the establishment realise that this would only be a qualitatitive change in the nature of their power, not a loss of power. A great deal of time may elapse before the others realise this. Self-managing enterprises and economic reform may mean a partial loss of power, but it may also mean the emergence of more stable authority, without which no modern society can function.

WŁODZIMIERZ PAŃKÓW

The Solidarity Movement, Management and the Political System in Poland

First of all, let us recap on the major events in recent Polish history. In early July 1980 the government announced price rises on some food items, particularly meat and meat products. This decision gave rise to a series of strikes in different parts of the country, including Lublin and Warsaw, which took place throughout July and into the beginning of August. On 14 August a strike broke out in the Lenin Shipyard in Gdańsk, the site of worker protests in December 1970. Workers in scores of enterprises in the region, and later in hundreds of enterprises in the Gdańsk, Szczecin, Słupsk and Elbląg regions and elsewhere came out on strike in support of Gdańsk. Soon these local protests assumed the characteristics of a general strike coordinated by the Inter-enterprise Strike Committee set up in the Gdańsk Shipyard. The Committee was headed by a former worker at the shipyard who had been dismissed for union activity. He was an electrician and his name was Lech Wałęsa. The information bulletin put out by the Gdańsk Shipyard bore the name 'Solidarity'.

In view of the scale of the protests and the speed with which they were spreading, the authorities decided to negotiate both with the Inter-enterprise Strike Committee of the Lenin Shipyard and another protest coordination centre, that in the Warski Shipyard in Szczecin. Among other things, these negotiations resulted in the setting up of an independent self-managed trade union which a few weeks later was given the title Solidarity.

The agreements negotiated in Gdańsk and Szczecin and then in the 'July Manifesto' Coalmine provided the basis for establishing

This text is inspired by the research into the independent self-managed trade union Solidarity by a Polish-French team under the guidance of Alain Touraine (see Touraine et al. 1983).

the structures of a national trade union which within a year had attracted to itself the majority of the country's employed workers, that is 9.5 million persons. During the first stage of its existence, the union's structures were founded on the Enterprise and Inter-enterprise strike committees which had been appointed by the respective workforces. In the summer of 1981, when the union had acquired some strength and had proved itself capable of meeting social expectations as well as defending its own existence — as after the 'Bydgoszcz events' — universal democratic elections were held to appoint the union's local and regional authorities. In September and October 1981 the union's programme was established and its authorities elected at Solidarity's First National Congress.

Martial law, which was imposed on 13 December 1981, brought Solidarity's open and legal existence to an end. In the weeks which followed, over 3 million workers went on strike.[1] A new chapter in the life of Solidarity had been opened.

In this chapter I would like to consider the purposes and functions of Solidarity in the system of political and economic domination which exists in Poland. In my view this is essential for an understanding of the events which took place in Poland in the period between the hot, hopeful days of August 1980 and the frosty, desperate and humiliating time in December 1981.

The first item to appear in the agreement concluded on 31 August 1980 between the Government Commission and the Inter-enterprise Strike Committee stated that 'it is acknowledged as desirable that there be called into being new, self-managed trade unions which would be an authentic *representative of the working class*' (emphasis added) and that 'the new trade unions will defend the *social* and material interests of the workers, and do not intend to perform the function of a political party' since 'the Polish United Workers' Party fulfils the leading role in the state' (original emphasis).[2]

As in the case of every settlement which has been reached by way of compromise, these formulations contain quite a number of inconsistencies and contradictions. It is hard to understand what they mean, or the meaning of individual concepts, without reference

1. 'According to information given by Professor Reykowski, PRON (see p. 19, n. 14) activist, at a conference of Party-member sociologists in Serock, 1983.
2. Records of the Gdańsk, Szczecin and Jastrzębie Agreements, Krajowa Agencja Wydawnicza, Warsaw, 1981, p. 2.

to the agreement as a whole.

In the first place, it is worth noting that the new trade unions which a few weeks later were to come to be known as Solidarity were not to represent some category or other of workers, but to represent the 'working class'. Within a year the majority of the 'working class' — a total of between 12.5 million and 13 million people if one also includes the peasants — acknowledged the new unions as their representative. As the authentic representative of the 'working class' the unions in fact stopped being unions and became a massive 'labour party' without the formal authority to perform party functions. Nevertheless, in representing the *social* and material interests of the 'working class' the unions did actually perform the function of a political party, even though they could not claim a share in the exercising of state authority. State authority was then in the hands of a 'party' which was not recognised by most of the 'working class' as their representative and which was losing any ability to represent society. Solidarity had this ability but could not put it to any use.

It was this paradox, exacerbated by the economic crisis, which determined the conditions under which Solidarity had to operate during the sixteen months which are of interest to us here. The absence of any other authentic representatives of society or the 'working class' and the difficulties involved in representation determined the demands articulated by the unions. But the limitations imposed by the economic situation and the August agreements — and more broadly, by the 'principles of the system' — made it impossible for these demands to be met. For these reasons Solidarity not only had to be a 'new-type union' but also had to be organised as a *social movement* with highly differentiated and complex objectives and functions. The strategy of the movement is evidence of a high degree of rationality. Its participants and leaders based nearly all their conclusions on past experience and made great allowances for the situation in which the movement operated. The demands which were made also had a rational basis. The events which took place after 13 December do not contradict this view, although short-term tactics may not have always conformed to the pattern.

Among other things, postwar Polish history may be considered as a sequence of events which rid society of its illusions with regard to the possibility of reforming the system of social organisation. The events of the Polish Summer followed a series of 'socialist renewals', the effects of which are well known. But with the Polish Summer came the Great Awakening. When one analyses the content of the demands submitted by the workforces in Gdańsk, Szczecin and Jastrzębie they emerge as the articulation of needs and social interests, in line with worker demands in December 1970. However, there were also a number of elements which took for granted the revolutionary nature of the agreements, particularly in the case of Gdańsk.

To start with, though this is not the most important aspect of the matter, the demands and agreements in the main referred to the needs and social interests of the whole of the 'working class', or to be precise, the major section of employed people except for the Party and the apparatus of repression. Thus in themselves the agreements became acts which articulated the interests of the newly formed 'working class'. The authorities' partners in the negotiations in this way made only minimal claims to represent the particular interests of any occupational category. This was most striking in the agreements concluded in Jastrzębie. The authorities, in the person of representatives of the state administration and members of the Party apparatus, had talks there with representatives of the Polish 'working class'. This meant a breaking of the monopoly of the Party, known as the Workers' Party, in the representation of the gainfully employed. It also meant that the 'working class' were disinvested of the illusion, still prevalent in October and even in December, that there existed in the Polish political system an organisation which could represent its interests after the appropriate 'democratisation' or 'renewal' processes had been set in motion.

For these reasons the August agreements contained demands for the reconstruction of the system responsible for the political and economic crisis, in addition to those relating to social and economic needs. In essence, these demands sought to ensure the basic conditions for the self-determination of the whole of Polish society. In setting up trade unions which were independent of the Party-state apparatus and demanding that they and their basic strike weapon be approved, the representatives of the 'working class' made it clear that they no longer had any illusions concerning the possibility of getting anywhere through the 'good-will' of the authorities. Pressure had to be exerted by the rank and file. It was emphasised that this had to be a continual and institutionalised pressure which could not be released at the point where it became inconvenient for the authorities. The agreements therefore put great emphasis on the provision of legal and institutional guarantees for *free social communication*. This was the basic condition for society to be able to integrate and organise itself, as well as the prerequisite for the effective social control of the activities of the authorities and their representatives.

In approving the independent trade unions and then reluctantly their activities, the authorities created a precedent which was hazardous both for themselves and the whole of the social organisational system referred to as the 'socialist state'. The precedent involved breaking the Party-state monopoly for organisational initiatives. In approving this precedent under tremendous social pressure, the apparatus accepted the right of people to *form associations* outside the direct supervision of this apparatus. Considering the logic of the system, this was a fact of considerable social significance since it allowed the possibility of the existence of authentic forms of social self-organisation alongside the 'social' organisations which were branches of the polymorphic Party. Such authentic forms of organisation might have served as bases from which ever wider areas of social life might have been liberated from Party-state domination.

Because of this, the August agreements were not simply the articulation of the interests of the major sectors of the 'working class' but also a draft for changes to the system leading to the institutionalisation of processes which would be responsive to social interests. The very formation of independent trade unions and their subsequent legalisation, became the first essential act of economic reform. The basic guidelines of this reform were laid out at the beginning of the agreements. Elsewhere in the agreements (Point 12 of the Gdańsk 'Records') another central question for economic reform was raised, namely the issue of *nomenklatura*. The above point demanded and approved that appointments to managerial positions would be made 'on the basis of qualifications and not Party membership'.[3]

The fact that demands were made which related to politics, the economy and the standard of living — in that order — as is illustrated by the Gdańsk Agreement in particular, shows that the representatives of the 'working class' had drawn all the necessary conclusions regarding the system which existed in Poland before August 1980. It is also proof of the rationality of the social movement which sprung to life in the coastal shipyards and the coalmines of Silesia in that month. It was a movement and not a trade union, for what trade union *sets out* with postulates of a political and general economic

3. Ibid., p. 6.

nature? The fact that the movement had to assume the organisational form of a trade union was not because of what it essentially was, but rather because of the conditions under which it came into being. This does not mean, however, that the movement did not *also* possess the essential characteristics of a trade union. That it did have these additional characteristics is confirmed, among other things, by the fact that after more than a year of its existence, the majority of Poles said they had no reservations with regard to its activities in the workplace while only about 14 per cent evaluated these activities negatively.[4] This result shows that the movement had a reliable social base which was mainly in the large enterprises.

It is also true that within a very short period of time the movement-union came to constitute a special kind of *organisational defence* which acted as a buffer for Polish society against the abuses of the power apparatus and the effects of the crisis. It did this by putting into practice the ideas which came into being in the second half of the 1970s, including those which had been circulated by the Workers' Committee of Self-defence, KOR. This represented a specific form of self-organisation on the part of society which the sociologist Jan Szczepański has termed the '*real state*', as opposed to the '*nominal state*' represented by the Party-state apparatus. The special nature of this 'real state' consisted among other things in the fact that although it had achieved a 'governance of souls' within a fairly short period of time as far as members of the 'ruling-class' — the majority of active society — were concerned, real state power remained outside its grasp. This actual 'governance of souls' allowed a kind of control to be exercised over the workplaces, primarily by the rank and file. However, it did not give economic control on a scale which would have allowed the country to be steered out of the crisis. In effect, although the creation of Solidarity structures nationwide provided the institutional preconditions for establishing the socioeconomic interests of the basic social groups, the probability that these interests would be realised did not increase to any significant extent. This was due to two inextricably linked factors: (a) the deep economic recession and (b) the rules by which the state and economy functioned and function, and which were at the root of the recession.

4. *Polacy '81* (The Poles in 1981), a study carried out by a team at the Polish Academy of Sciences Institute of Philosophy and Sociology under the guidance of W. Adamski in November and December 1981 (Adamski, Beskid et al. 1982).

The ever more keenly felt systemic blockade against acting in accordance with these interests accounts for the dynamics of the movement during 1981. It explains, in particular, the changing interests, postulates and demands put forward by the majority of participants and activists and the changes in the people to whom they were directed. As I have already mentioned, the demands which had been made in August related to the functioning of the political system, the economy and the standard of living (i.e. wages, welfare benefits and conditions of employment). To meet these demands would have been to act towards the implementation of the central norms and values espoused for centuries by progressive social movements in Europe and America. These include the independence of society, the sovereignty of the individual and the nation, prosperity, social justice, equality of rights, duties and opportunity, tolerance and so on. The national and religious symbols of the Solidarity movement which were present from the outset, indicates that is has a fourth essential dimension, that of national and state independence and cultural separateness. In the first few weeks, this could be seen in the banners, portraits, songs and religious behaviour, and also appeared in the point in the agreements dealing with religion in the mass media. This dimension became increasingly prominent in its activities, but increasingly the movement's objectives were blocked. This aspect received spectacular, though in my opinion impractical, expression in the 'Message to East European Nations' at the Solidarity's First National Congress in September 1981.

The four aspects of the movement which we have singled out — that is those relating to trade union activity and living standards, economic reform, political democratisation and national independence — co-existed between August 1980 and December 1981.[5] They created four dimensions, a social, economic, political and geopolitical one, each of which directly and indirectly affected the changes which determined what could be achieved in the dimension which preceded it. In other words, the state of the economy determined the limits to what could be achieved with regard to welfare and living standards; the existing and essentially untouched political system set the limit for essential economic reform, while the chances of change in both these dimensions were more or less directly determined by external pressures. That is to say, the reali-

5. This is a modified version of the typology introduced by Touraine et al. (1983).

117

sation of the interests articulated in the Agreements and in local agreements required radical reforms which would encompass the institutional, material and property structure of the economy, and this was not feasible if no essential changes were to be made to the political system. From the point of view of the movement's expectations and objectives, it might be said that changes in these three dimensions were to some degree and at a certain point in time, *equivalent*. For example, essential political changes could have been treated as a guarantee for a postponed improvement of the economy and living standards. However, significant changes in these three dimensions would have entailed a reduction in external pressures, which, as was to become clear very soon, was out of the question.

In my opinion three stages of the official existence of the movement can be distinguished: (a) from August 1980 to late March 1981, (b) from March 1981 to late September 1981 and (c) from late September 1981 until the introduction of martial law. The dimensions we have enumerated were not always apparent to the same extent, and the forms in which they revealed themselves varied. This was largely the result of a process of learning on the part of the movement, or more precisely, on the part of the participants of the movement. Changes occurred as conclusions were drawn from experience but at the same time were influenced by the movement's original aims. To oversimplify, one might refer to the three phases of the movement's open existence as the *syndical* or union phase, the *economic* phase and the *political* phase, respectively.

I do not refer to the first phase as syndical because a struggle was taking place at the time for the setting up and legalisation of the NSZZ Solidarity. This activity was clearly of a political nature; however, this was politics on an elementary yet vital level, for what was at stake were the basic conditions for society's right to self-determination — the right to form associations, to communicate freely and so on. The movement-union which was coming into being kept its distance from problems relating to the internal functioning of the political system and did not demand any reform of the ruling party or any change in the ruling team. Thus it broke with the illusions so typical of previous 'renewals' since it considered itself to be *the only guarantor* of the interests of the 'working class'. On the economic front, the movement obliged the Party-state apparatus to undertake work on economic reforms, but at the same time explicitly refused to share any of the responsibility for the economy, which was then in a very poor way. Rather, its participants concentrated on what Wałęsa has referred to as 'small-scale clean-ups'.

Apart from the setting-up and legalising of formal union structures, during the syndical phase most of the participants' energy was taken up by *collective claims* aimed at revealing and realising the interests, particularly material interests, of different socio-professional groups. As a result of these actions, hundreds of agreements were signed in ministries, at regional level, and at workplaces. In these agreements the representatives of the Party-state and economic apparatus undertook to meet thousands of demands which expressed the needs and interests of different groups of the 'working class'. Commitments of a financial nature were made and carried out fairly readily. Although this contributed to the destruction of the market which was in trouble in any case, it did not in any way impinge on the interests of the power apparatus. It was simply a continuation of the practices during Gierek's period in the 1970s whereby different groups of workers were bribed in order to maintain social peace. Wherever the interests of any section of the power apparatus were involved, it was much more difficult to achieve agreement, as was clearly confirmed by the events in the Bielsko-Biała voivodeship.

The climax of this first phase was the fight for free Saturdays. As in the case of the monetary claims, after some pressure had been brought to bear, the demands were more or less met. However, in the following months it became obvious that syndical action brings limited results and confronts major obstacles. It grew clear that in an economy which functioned with disregard for the rules and criteria of economic efficiency, collective claims, either with regard to pay or hours, *do not result in a rationalisation of production processes* as in the case of economies based on price-market mechanisms. The rise in labour costs and the reduction in man-hours did not make those in charge of the economy look for other ways of lowering costs or raising productivity. The Party-state apparatus was busy 'renewing' and 'purging' itself and had almost entirely lost the ability to coordinate action in the economy, confining itself to blocking actions which it considered to be a threat to its own position. There followed a kind of decentralisation of responsibility for the hardship which was by then being caused by many objective factors such as shortages of power, raw materials, spare parts and so on. Management was only beginning to learn how to co-exist and collaborate with the new element in the production process, that is the independent trade unions. In all, the economy was increasingly unable to boost the supply of commodities and services.

With a rapidly increasing deficit of essential goods, and with the limited investment capacity of the enterprises, typically syndical actions such as claims for increased wages, reduced working hours or improved working conditions, gradually ceased to make sense. It was becoming clear that given the state of the economy, they might lead to its eventual destruction. On the other hand, a section of the power apparatus was recovering from the shock of the movement's initial success, and in the second half of March 1981 it made a first attempt to check the movement's impetus. The full details of what are known as the 'Bydgoszcz events' are not known to this day, but there is much to indicate that they represented the beginning of a push to restore the order which existed prior to August 1980. This was prevented by the efficient action of the movement-union, and by signs of a revolt at the 'base' of the ruling Party. At that time, a considerable section of that base had formed the movement of so-called horizontal structures and was involved in a struggle for the democratisation of Party and state life.

Although the movement had been saved, the March crisis meant changes in the way it functioned. It brought a transition to the second phase, which I have termed the 'economic' phase. Before going on to discuss this phase, I would like to draw attention to some of the main lessons learnt from the Bydgoszcz events.

The attempt which was made then to attack the union and the movement weakened the idea, which had been popular just after August 1980, of reform of the power system in Poland. According to this idea, the power apparatus would be reconciled to the existence of a legalised 'workers' opposition' which would assure that the rank and file of workers would be able to exercise control over the power apparatus. The events of March were a clear signal that significant elements of the Party-state apparatus would not agree with that specific 'social democratic' concept of a power system which Wałęsa had summed up as 'keeping the authorities on a leash'.

The first significant event to prompt the union to reorientate its activities as it so clearly did in the second quarter of 1981, had been the disclosure in January by a government department of the guidelines to the planned economic reforms. It became obvious to many of the participants in the movement and to independent experts that the reform was too serious a matter to leave to the officials. The reform guidelines which were published by the Commission for Economic Reform only went halfway in such essential matters as the independence and self-management of enterprises, while the matter of self-financing was dealt with in a most perfunctory way. What caused particular concern was the fact that the document was silent over the matter of the role of the Party apparatus and organisations in economic management. There were some signals, both in the document and in the pronouncements of the Party leadership, which led people to assume that no essential changes were intended in this regard. Going by past experience, which had been largely negative, it was possible to predict what this might mean for reform and the future of the economy.

The rapidly worsening economic situation, the movement's disappointment with the achievements of the syndical stage, the authorities' violent defence against the rank and file gaining control of its actions, and the incomplete and inconsistent plan for economic reform — all these factors were responsible for bringing about the movement's gradual reorientation in its efforts at achieving a radical change in the rules governing the functioning of the economy. Because of the nature of the system, it is clear that actions aimed at economic reform, mainly *reform of the ownership system*, were not only of an economic but also of a *political* character, since they entailed a curtailment of the power of the Party-state and the Party as a whole. Despite this, I refer to the second phase of the movement's existence as the economic phase. These activities were pursued until December 1981, although by late September they had assumed a minor role. On the political plane, these activities signified that the movement had passed from the 'social democratic' approach involving the defence of the interests of the working class and the control of the authorities by the rank and file, to attempts to *limit and divide power*.

One way of radically curtailing the power of the Party, and the Party apparatus in particular, over economic organisation was to be widespread worker self-management. It was to achieve its aims by: (a) eliminating or at least radically limiting the *nomenklatura* system; (b) appointing a new employer — the workers' council or a director elected by that council — who would be independent of the Party-state bureaucracy; (c) ensuring the influence of the workforce on how the income from their work was to be divided; and (d) limiting or eliminating the role of Party organisations in the operational management of economic organisations; one-person management would be exercised by a director appointed and controlled by self-management bodies, and not as previously through 'collective management'.

This kind of self-management could not be instituted overnight. The development of concepts of self-management and the involvement of the movement in their realisation continued throughout 1981 until the declaration of martial law. It is notable that although actions supporting worker self-management were initiated, inspired and nurtured by Solidarity, most of such actions took place outside the union itself, thus forming another stream in the movement alongside the trade unionist one. Most of the action supporting worker autonomy — for example, the development of ideas of self-government, the formulation of the statutes of self-governing bodies, the formulation of a legal framework for their operation and the organisation of elections to these bodies — was carried out by the union's Enterprise Commissions. A considerable section of union activists, particularly those at regional and central level, expressed some reservations about this action, maintaining that it would weaken the union by siphoning off the energy needed for effective union operation. They argued that if workers participated in the appointment of their employers, the trade union would have to share *responsibility* for the consequences of their decisions, and thus it would also be indirectly responsible for the past decisions of the political apparatus in the economy.

In spite of these doubts and differences in approach, most of the movement-union activists at the 'base', that is at the workplace, were saying as early as June that worker autonomy was what could unite them. This emerged in the study conducted by a research team under the guidance of Touraine et al. (1983). On the other hand, a survey of the opinions of union members carried out in August 1981 showed that the rank and file had a limited interest in economy, while the decisions taken in September of that year indicate a lack of determination at the top of the union-movement.[6] Meanwhile the debates of the Ninth Congress of the Polish United Workers' Party showed there was much determination in the opposing camp; the ruling Party decided to defend its position in the economy, both at central and enterprise level. The Seym, acting according to the wishes of the Party, drew up legislation relating to

6. According to a survey of the opinions of union members in the Solidarity region 'Mazovia' in August 1981.

state enterprises, and the self-management of such enterprises thus became the Party's main instrument of defence. The effect of this disintegration of interests was the 'rotten compromise' of September, considered by most activists to represent the defeat of the movement. The legislation which was passed deferred the issue of the autonomy of economic organisations. Thus the Party defended its position in the economy in an incomplete fashion, and one which was likely to give rise to future conflict. Meanwhile the movement participants began increasingly to share the doubts as to the possibility of reforming the rules governing the economy without vital changes to the rules governing 'purely' political life. As a result of the experiences of the first two phases of the movement's existence, this doubt gradually changed to certainty and led to the third, political phase.

Disappointment among movement participants was not only caused by the failure to institutionalise and legitimise the model of worker self-management which had been developed by the so-called 'Network'. Several events during the movement's second phase indicated that a considerable section of the power apparatus viewed the agreements signed between August and March as a kind of subterfuge. The second phase was concerned with the implementation of these agreements. It became clear to everyone that almost none of the postulates formulated by the movement in August 1980 and later had been implemented without pressure having to be exerted. This did not apply to monetary hand-outs, but it was particularly conspicuous with regard to the provision of preconditions for free social communication; this would have meant a break of the Party-state's monopoly over the mass media. The ruling Party, which is supported by 11 per cent of 'society',[7] probably largely Party members, had almost complete control over the mass media with both censorship and repressive measures at their disposal. The Party made no concessions whatsoever with regard to non-state control over the mass information media. It also effectively counteracted the attempts made by the movement to introduce social control over food production and distribution. There was good reason for this, for it considered this to be the first step in the weakening of the Party's power in the economy.

A section of the movement's participants and activists set their hopes on the Special Ninth Conference of the Polish United Work-

7. Adamski, Beskid et al. (1982).

ers' Party, which finally took place in mid-July 1981. These hopes had been encouraged by the movement within the Party for horizontal structures; this position involved among other things essential changes in the function and position of the Party in the state, economy and society. The letter from the Central Committee of the Communist Party of the Soviet Union dated June 1981, and the ensuing actions of the Polish Party apparatus, put a stop to such tendencies, and the outcome of the Ninth Congress did not differ significantly from the outcome of previous gatherings. The programme for dealing with the crisis which was put forward at the Congress was once more to be the 'programme of the nation', and even according to the 'liberal' faction of the Central Committee's Politburo, in the person of K. Barcikowski, the only obstacle to this goal was Solidarity, which caused a split between Party and society. However, the same Party leader was already noticing signs that the movement's influence was waning, and he linked this to the opportunity for quickly establishing a dialogue between the Party and society. The whole course of events from then till now has been the result of the application of these concepts relating to the wielding of power by the Party. It was neglect of the fact that Solidarity was no barrier between the authorities and society, but rather a *form of organisation of that society* which accounted for the construction of such groundless concepts as the 'silent majority' and in effect for the actions which constituted 'martial law' in Poland. Of course, it cannot be ruled out that the result of the huge grinding mill which was put into operation on 13 December 1981 will not be a ground down 'silent majority', but it is certain that the apparatus of the new-type Party has striven and will strive for a 'majority' which is silent and submissive. However, there is danger in the fact that people who are unable to speak are often thought to be unable to hear.

The toughness of the authorities' stance towards the movement was strengthened by a greater sense of representativeness of the Party authorities which had been recently appointed by democratic election. This could be seen in the course of the negotiations which were held between the Presidium of the Agreement Committee and the Government Trade Union Committee in the first ten days of August. During the talks the government replied to the union's seven postulates, which were strictly within the terms of the August Agreements, by coming up with twelve demands of their own aimed at 'dismantling Solidarity', as Wałęsa put it. These demands clearly revealed the authorities' desire to incorporate into the union many of the aspects of the former Central Council of Trade Unions. Nothing was fixed during these talks, but at a meeting on 12 August Solidarity's Agreement Committee made a formal appeal to union members to take an active part in overcoming the crisis which had been caused by the 'system of economic management and state rule'. The Agreement Committee appealed to union members to work eight free Saturdays, to support worker self-management and to refrain from protest marches and sporadic strikes. In this, Solidarity clearly exceeded trade union activity and assumed responsibility both for the course of events in the workplace and in the economy as a whole.

This reorientation of the movement-union was not greeted with joy by the government, nor did it welcome the resolution concerning the movement's programme of action which had been carried at Solidarity's First National Congress, and which went far beyond a purely unionist formula. From August 1981 onwards, the Party-government's propaganda attacks on the movement's activities intensified, as did the use of repressive measures. In the case of the former a climax was reached with the 'Radom Watergate', and in the case of the latter, with the quelling of the strike at the Officers' Fire-fighting School in Warsaw. In the successive rounds of the negotiations which ensued, the government assumed an increasingly dismissive attitude towards the union. This was most conspicuous in the talks which were held in mid-November with reference to issues connected with economic reform. There is much evidence that from August 1981 onwards the government was preparing to abolish the 'obstacle' — that is, Solidarity — which in their view prevented society from wishing to cooperate with it. On 14 September A. Siwak, a member of the newly elected Politburo, stated at a meeting with newsmen that the delegalisation of Solidarity should be considered, and that 'they had enough people in the Security Service and in the army to deal with that'.[8]

Officially, however, the representatives of the Party-state apparatus promoted the idea of the Front of National Understanding. In practice this meant putting up election lists which had been finalised with the Polish United Workers' Party and approved by it, for the elections to People's Councils which were to be held in the early

---

8. According to a report in *Independence*, the daily newspaper of the Solidarity region 'Mazovia', 17 September 1981.

spring. Attempts were also made to involve Solidarity representatives in different commissions which were working on important social matters and which had been set up by the authorities. The idea of these mixed commissions and the Committees of National Agreement with limited union representation alongside representatives of the Party and other political parties and associations, was to be a way of *co-opting and adjusting* the movement-union to the existing political system, always under the key control of the Polish United Workers' Party.

The union leaders represented the overwhelming majority of the working class and were not interested in the idea of a national agreement which assumed that they represented only a limited section of the population. They were increasingly orientated to political changes which, on the one hand, would facilitate radical economic reforms and, on the other, would lead to the realisation of the idea of a 'self-managing republic'.

From September 1981 onwards there was an increasing number of political elements in the postulates and actions of the movement. Some of them were obvious within Solidarity structures; purely political actions such as the attempts to set up political clubs and parties took place outside the union but under its wing. In sum, it may be said that the union-movement became an organised *'political force'* after its First Congress. As such it had a fairly centralised structure and the capacity for disciplined action directed from above which could exercise pressure in talks between the union and its recalcitrant opponent. This concept of the union-movement was supported by Wałęsa and a considerable section of his advisors and was to ensure the channelling of the spontaneous actions of the rank and file which could have been useful in the political game which the union was playing. At the same time, however, it might have paralysed the self-management initiative which was revived after August 1980 and which is the essence of any social movement. Who can tell whether it was not this which explains the relatively easy success of the forces of repression in December 1981?

This organisational model of a 'political force' taking part in a game assumes that the rules of the game are observed by both sides; these rules do not necessarily exclude bluff, as for example in the union leaders' Radom declaration. However, when one's adversary uses methods which trangress these rules, this organisational model may prove of little use.

These observations are corroborated by the fact that the movement's aim was to limit and divide the power exercised by the Party-state apparatus, mainly as a result of the actions of the rank and file, not those higher up. This was because the idea of a coalition government where power would be shared by representatives from the three main political forces in the country — the Party, Solidarity and Catholic laymen — even if feasible in the light of geopolitical considerations, was not one which was trusted in the light of the events which took place during the years from 1945 to 1948. The meeting which took place in early November between Jaruzelski, Wałęsa and Glemp leads one to suppose that such an idea was under consideration, although some no doubt considered it more seriously than others. There remained the creation of self-management bodies, initially at enterprise and local level, and later at voivodeship level, possibly leading to the creation of a self-management chamber attached to the Seym. Nor were 'free' elections to the Seym in the future ruled out. Both the postulates submitted to the government in talks at central level and the actions of a section of the movement's activists and advisors indicated that it was this orientation which prevailed in the movement by the autumn of 1981. This was confirmed in a study carried out among movement activists in mid-November 1981.[9] This approach was associated with strongly held views with regard to Poland's autonomy. The prevalent attitude among those interviewed was that without 'socialisation' of the state, and in particular of the People's Councils and the Seym, full economic reform would be impossible. As is known, at that time the movement declared itself in favour of a partial version of such 'socialisation', that is the appointment of a Social Council for the National Economy which was to both consult and control the government and act as representative of social organisations and powerful social groups.

The formation of a Social Council for the National Economy and the drafting of a new law governing elections to the people's councils and then for the Seym were among the postulates formulated by Solidarity's National Commission and put forward during talks with government representatives which were initiated in mid-November 1981. If the demands were not met within three months, the Commission threatened a general strike. It goes without saying that if the demands had been met, the Party would have lost control over the traditional state institutions — the Seym, the government,

9. Touraine et al. (1983).

the people's councils and regional administration. Taken together with the expansion of self-management, despite legal obstacles, and the pressure to do away with central distribution as the basis for the management of the economy, a situation was created which presented the Party with two options. Either it could share power, receiving in return a guarantee concerning its constitutional role in society, or it could try to destroy or at least weaken the adversary which had put it in this difficult position. The first option was risky, and moreover it involved a breaking of the 'universal rules of socialism' which had never in any case been fully observed in Poland. It was therefore an option which was unacceptable to the headquarters of the camp, as well as the local commanders. The other option involved severe social and economic losses, but in the long term it might have lead to the operation of those 'universal rules of socialism'. This was the genesis of martial law in Poland, introduced on 13 December 1981, on the day of St Lucia — patron saint of the blind.

What has been said above concerning the structure and dynamics of the movement and what I have found to be the signs of rationality in the movement, refers in the main to its *strategy*. I believe that at this level the movement's participants formulated the objectives which were derived both from the logic of the system in which the movement came into being and from the nature of the situation in which Poland found itself. The above-mentioned dimensions of the movement and the changes of content and meaning within the different phases of its existence are in my view proof of its ability to reach the right conclusions on the basis of experience. It does not mean, however, that we should not ask, in the light of the experience of the Great Polish Awakening, how much sense there is in this kind of phased, self-limiting revolution. What we can ask is, if a similar movement is to be successful in a similar system, whether some of these phases should be rearranged or eliminated. In other words, would it not have been possible to try to bring everything to a close in August–September 1980 or in March 1981? These are not simply theoretical or historical questions.

The positive evaluation of the movement with regard to strategy does not extend to the level of tactics, that is to the realisation of strategic goals. Here a number of errors were made, including the following: (1) Factions of the movement allowed the adversary to involve them in diversionary conflicts of minor importance. (2) The adversary was often treated too much as a homogeneous entity. Allies should have been made in order to achieve specific goals. For example, management should have been won over to the ideas of economic reform, which would have been advantageous both to the economy in general and themselves in particular. (3) There was sometimes a lack of consistency in the achievement of specific objectives, for example the case of worker self-management. (4) The strike weapon was relied upon too frequently as a form of pressure. It is effective against those whose own profit is threatened, but there is no evidence that there is a close relationship between the withdrawal of labour by a 'socialist worker' and the threatening of the interests of the 'socialist employer'. (5) The avant-garde moved too far away from the body of the movement. This influenced the movement's perception of the aims which the avant-garde formulated and thus reduced the probability that they would be achieved.

These are just a few of the tactical errors which were made. To them may be added phenomena which invariably accompany mass movements, for example the formation of an oligarchy, bureaucratisation, centralisation and the formation of factions. To be fair it should be said that these were perceived and analysed by the movement, which does not mean to say that the phenomena were eliminated or under control. However, the fact that after fourteen months of the existence of the movement only between 14 and 16 per cent of Poles judged the effects of its activity in the workplace and in the country as a whole, to be negative, shows that these aspects were not exceedingly significant.[10] The other point is that these judgements were also influenced by the wider context within which the movement-union was active.

10. Adamski, Beskid et al. (1982).

MIRA MARODY

Social Stability and the Concept of Collective Sense

For years the aspect of social consciousness on which Polish sociologists have concentrated their attention has been that concerned with attitudes and values.[1] If one is interested in the links between these attitudes and values and reality, empirical data is mainly to be interpreted in terms of the degree of acceptance which the current social and political system enjoys in Poland. The level of this acceptance would seem to be rather low, regardless of whether one bases this judgement on direct or more indirect data. The most direct question which has been put in this regard is: 'Would you like the world to move in the direction of the kind of socialism which exists in Poland?' Here, affirmative answers ranged from 4 per cent [2] to 20.5 per cent.[3] The percentage of 'definitely in favour' responses varied correspondingly from 3.3 to 0.6.

The low level of acceptance of the social and political system also manifests itself more indirectly. For example, students were twice as likely to choose life options which lay 'outside or alongside the system' (e.g. a temporary stay abroad, running a private workshop, going on childcare leave) as they were options within the institutional order (i.e. full-time work). When asked, 'Which country would you live in if you had the choice?', only 60 per cent of

I would like to express my thanks to my colleagues from the Department of Methodology at the Institute of Sociology, University of Warsaw, and also to A. Rychard and J. Poleszczuk. Their comments on a preliminary draft of this chapter were invaluable in helping me to clarify the present version.

1. This text is based on an analysis of over twenty studies, most of them carried out in 1983–4. I shall refer to them in the notes below. The data serve of course as an illustration and not proof of my theoretical hypotheses.

2. Lindenberg 1986 (study) — students at Warsaw University and Warsaw Technical University; N=650.

3. Krasucki, Nowak and Mierzwińska (1984) — workers from a large and small enterprise in Warsaw; N=1,020.

students mentioned Poland. Finally, when presented with a list of system features, respondents only selected negatively evaluated characteristics to refer to the present Polish system. These included such characteristics as a strong highly centralised government apparatus taking decisions on all vital issues, restrictions on the activities of opponents of the government or — though this was seen as a less important issue — the existence, for example, of state-controlled industry.[4]

This lack of acceptance is also decisive in the evaluation of more specific elements of the system. Among state institutions only the Seym and the government were mentioned with over 50 per cent frequency by respondents as definitely or on the whole warranting the trust of society (60.5 and 51.8 per cent, respectively). [5] In other surveys 4.2 per cent of workers and 1.6 per cent of intellectuals thought that the Seym 'enjoyed very great confidence'; for the government the figures were 2.7 and 0 per cent, respectively.[6] These were the highest scoring institutions.[7]

On a theoretical level the acceptance or lack of acceptance of the social and political system are usually examined in terms of legitimisation or legality — terms identified with 'credibility'. In this approach a given social and political system is legitimised if the majority of society believes that it is fair and just. This belief is usually based on a consistency between the values which are observed by the people on the one hand and observed in practice by the system on the other (Lipset 1959; Habermas 1979). In the light of the data which are cited above, one might say — and it often has been — that the Polish system is perceived as illegitimate, that is, as lacking in credibility in the eyes of society.

This kind of approach to legitimisation does not, however, provide a convenient concept for the description of Polish reality. There are two reasons for this. In the first place, in practice it only covers the realm of attitudes and values and does not allow for a description of the realm of action. In particular, the theory of legitimisation implicitly assumes a correspondence between the sphere of values and the sphere of action. 'A crisis of legitimacy is a crisis of change', Lipset (1959) has written, while in Weber's (1975)

---

4. See notes 2 and 3.
5. CBOS (Centre for Social Opinion Studies) data, 1984; national sample.
6. CBOS data, April–June 1984; intelligentsia (N=673) and workers (N=697) from Poland's seven largest cities.
7. With the exception of the Church. Corresponding data for the Church were 82.4 per cent (see note 5) and 35.1 per cent (see note 6).

131

classic work the term 'legitimation' is introduced to explain motives of *obedience*, that is motives of conformity between actions and the norms imposed by the social order. Thus the absence of legitimisation is a concept which allows us to explain actions whose aim is to change the social and political system. However, it is useless when, as in Poland, the rejection of the system occurs primarily in the symbolic realm of views and opinions, for the lack of acceptance expressed in many studies does not at present often go hand in hand with actions which aim to transform the system. On the contrary, it is possible to observe behaviour which positively supports or at least does not undermine the system, although this does not necessarily result from an acceptance of the system.

In the second place, in this specific case reference to the concept of legitimation forces us implicitly or explicitly to accept what I would call the 'oppressive theory of society'. For the central explanation of the inconsistencies between symbol and action is sought in a system of political and police control; that is, it involves a conceptualisation of society in categories of enslavement. For this reason the concept of legitimation is rejected by many writers who regard legitimation as neither a necessary nor sufficient condition for the stability of a social order. Since the existence of a particular social order always, with the exception of military occupation, requires some form of acceptance on the part of society or the majority of that society, these writers distinguish certain forms of passive acceptance which derive their legitimating force from what might generally be referred to as the institutional fit or institutional involvement in the social order (Mann 1975). This is the sense in which Rychard (1984) uses the term 'acquiescence', that is the acceptance of a system through the actions which are realised within it.

The concept of acquiescence, however, shares a certain drawback with that of legitimation, namely the fact that an important area of social life remains beyond its compass. This is the sphere of values. Moreover, in place of the 'oppressive theory of society' the concept of acquiescence introduces the 'accommodation theory of the individual', whereby the main motive power of human action is the satisfaction of individual interests and aspirations within the *existing* social and political formation.

We can therefore say that the two main concepts used to describe the relation of Polish society to the Polish social order 'lose' important elements of this relation. In practice the concept of legitimation excludes daily actions from its description while the concept of acquiescence excludes values. In consequence, the concept of legitimation, though it concentrates on problems of the stability of the social order, paradoxically does not form a basis for the explanation of the persistence of a specific type of order, while the concept of acquiescence, which stresses the flexibility of human behaviour, is less reliable when dealing with actions whose presumed aim is to change the social order.[8] For this reason I would like to put forward here the concept of the *collective sense* as one which allows us to describe stability and change in a social order while taking account of both values and social actions.[9]

The Concept of Collective Sense

I understand the collective sense to be a value or set of values whose realisation forms the basis for the passive or active acceptance of authority by society.[10] In other words, the collective sense marks out the sphere of specific consensus between the authorities and society. This consensus is a product of a 'bargaining' process in which the authorities undertake to introduce and maintain a type of social order which allows a given value to be realised, while society undertakes to submit to authority in the name of this value.[11] Thus the collective sense is a value which channels the collective effort of society and simultaneously forms the basis on which the social order is constructed and accepted.

This requires further explanation. First and foremost, it is obvious that the concept of collective sense does not exhaust the whole

8. We find a similar incongruence of concepts in Polish sociology where attitudes and values are interpreted on the level of meaning (Marody and Nowak 1983).
9. I have borrowed the concept of collective sense from Touraine (1984a, 1984b). His meaning is slightly different from mine.
10. I am aware that the distinction introduced here between 'society' and the 'authorities' is far from precise. Moreover, it may be very hard to operationalise, particularly as far as the lower levels of the political and administrative apparatus are concerned. Nevertheless, it would be difficult to do without this kind of distinction, since we are interested in the attitudes of people towards the social and political system within which they have to live. The object of human attitudes and opinions is rarely the abstract social and political system referred to by sociologists and political scientists. It is more often the people who hold power and institutions and their rules of behaviour. The term 'authorities' refers to all of these things.
11. The theoretical proposal suggested here may be regarded as an attempt to create a plane on which two major but distinct organising principles in human collectivities may be examined, that is the social principle and the political principle, or in other words the dimension of community and the dimension of subordination (Buber 1983). The terms 'bargaining', 'to undertake', 'negotiations' and other such personifications are obviously used metaphorically and not literally.

range of values and needs of society on the one hand (values and needs S) or those of the authorities on the other (values and needs A), although in practice the scope of the negotiated consensus may be broader than the conceptual scope of the values which constitute the collective sense. For despite the fact that the collective sense usually only includes only one or two S values, they are so general that their realisation through collective action can increase the chances of realising numerous individual desires and aspirations.[12] Similarly, the realisation by the authorities of the values which go to make up the collective sense is a guarantee at the very least of the passive acquiescence of the governed in being governed. At the very best, it engages the full cooperation of society in those actions of the authorities which aim to realise other A values and needs which are instrumental with respect to the collective sense. Regardless of the extent of consensus in practice, there can and usually do appear on both sides of this social relation, values which do not interest and may be rejected as hostile to the specific interests and needs of the other side. As a result, although the collective sense is a value which lends general direction to collective effort, explanations of specific collective and individual actions call for a consideration of both the remaining S values and needs which characterise the interests of society, as well as their relation to the values which make up the collective sense.[13]

The relation of the collective sense to the social order is similar. The social order is understood here to be a well-ordered and interconnected set of rules of action which are formally and/or actually operative in society. The main elements of this order are (a) norms of action and (b) institutions; these constitute the normative and institutional social order.[14] It is possible to distinguish two

12. In other words, the optimum situation from the standpoint of social development is the situation where the collective sense encompasses individual senses, i.e. where individual actions directed towards achieving individual aspirations together form the collective sense.

13. More precisely, an explanation of behaviour has to take more than values into account. To put it briefly, within the theory of action assumed here, behaviour is the result of the interaction of orientating factors such as values, attitudes and needs, and releasing factors such as belief in the adequacy of available means for achieving goals and a belief that opportunities exist constructed on the basis of the common knowledge of the individuals concerned. For a more detailed discussion of this see Marody (1987), Marody and Nowak (1983). The actions of the authorities and the A values underlying them are in the light of this formulation an element of the commonsense knowledge of individuals.

14. This definition is identical with that suggested by Sztompka (1983) concerning the normative structure of society. If I use a different term here it is because I wish to separate the formal framework of action, referred to here as the 'social order', from

types of social order: (a) an assumed social order which can be reconstructed by examining legal and declared cultural norms, regulations, statutes and so on, and (b) a realised social order, that is, the way in which people and institutions really function which sometimes differs quite considerably from the verbalisations of the assumed order. We are mainly interested here in the real state of affairs and will use the term 'social order' in this context.

I stated above that the social order is constructed on the basis of a value or set of values which form the collective sense. By this I mean that at least in its theoretical form norms of action and the institutional order should promote, or at least should not hinder, the realisation of the collective sense. However, the ultimate form a social order takes is determined, on the one hand, by the actions the authorities take to create an institutional framework which allows the realisation of A needs and A values which have not been covered by the negotiated consensus. On the other hand, it is determined by society's collective actions, which aim to realise those S values and needs which do not form part of the collective sense. These actions can lead to a form of social order which is dysfunctional with respect to the values which form the basis of the consensus, thus posing the problem of change to the authorities or to society.

Generally speaking, according to the approach suggested here, change can be initiated by three kinds of events. First, the basis for the consensus, i.e. the collective sense, can be socially 'invalidated'. This can happen when the target values which form the collective sense have been realised in absolute or relative terms. This occurs in the case of specific goals such as defence against incursion, national reconstruction following a war, the upward mobility of social groups which were the main 'signatories' of the consensus, and so on, or when a value which was previously valid is displaced by one which results from the failure to meet certain needs. Invalidation of the existing collective sense can also take place when a new generation assumes the major role in public life and has a different value system from the one espoused by the generation which is withdrawing from the public arena. In all of these cases the possibility of bargaining exists, during which a new collective sense may be

---

the values which determine the goals of this action. Sztompka includes these values in his concept of the normative structure of society. Apart from this difference, it seems to me that the theoretical suggestion which I put forward is complementary in many places to the theory of structural change which he presents, even though it is formulated on a different level.

created and with it a change in the social order.

Secondly, change may be initiated if the form the social order assumes turns out to be ineffective or even dysfunctional with respect to the value forming the basis of the consensus. I mentioned earlier that the process which modifies an existing social order is actually an in-built one; in other words, it is an integral part of the actual process of the construction of a social order. These modifications can, particularly when social forces are not in equilibrium, lead to a situation in which one of the sides in the 'national understanding' feels strong enough or sufficiently threatened to attempt to introduce or have introduced corrections to the social order which amount to a fundamental change, even if such a change consists of returning to the starting-point. This opens up a new stage of negotiations during which the collective sense may also be changed.

Finally, the social order can also be changed by force. When this is initiated by society, we usually speak of a revolution; when it is initiated by the authorities, we call it a *coup d'état*. This is then usually followed by a change in the collective sense, where a new social consensus is negotiated within the new arrangement of forces, or in the absence of such consensus the collective sense is shaped by obedience invoked by the use or threat of violence.

In sum, we can say that according to the approach adopted here one condition for the stability of the social order — understood in relative terms since the social order is in a continuous process of construction — is the existence of a consensus between society and the authorities, based on the collective sense.[15] Change in the social order may be initiated either through the value which forms the collective sense becoming 'extinct', through the order becoming dysfunctional with respect to the values and needs of one of the parties to the consensus, through force or, most probably, through a combination of these factors.[16]

Although the construction of and hence also change in the social order should be regarded as a continuous process, it is more

15. The stability of the social order can obviously be maintained by force. However, since it would be hard to talk of a social consensus in such a case, I shall not deal with it further in my argument. Incidentally, it is worth mentioning here that the consensus approach to the explanation of certain fragments of the social and political situation in Poland was recently used by Morawski (1980) and Reykowski (1985).

16. Factors initiating change should not be confused with the reasons for this change, where reasons are understood to be a set of phenomena and facts which *led up to* change.

convenient for purely technical reasons to analyse these problems by concentrating on moments of sudden crisis. From this point of view the postwar history of Polish *society* can be interpreted as a succession of collective senses and consequent changes in the social order.[17] During the period from 1945 to 1949 the collective sense which formed the basis of consensus between the authorities and society was the commonly espoused value of national reconstruction following the devastation of the war.[18] Towards the end of this period, however, the authorities were already making efforts to change the social order as witnessed by the political turn-around of 1948. This coincided with a relative weakening on the part of society of the value which made up the existing collective sense. The period 1949 to 1956 was that of the six-year plan; here the basis of consensus was the upward social mobility of a considerable section of society.[19]

The political events at the beginning of the period from 1956 to 1980 may be regarded both as an expression of the desire to change the existing social order as well as of the replacement of values which had formed the basis of the collective sense until then. The new social consensus was based on the values of economic development and the democratisation of social life. This period has two essential characteristics. In the first place, the value referred to as 'the democratisation of social life' underwent considerable evolution. Initially, it was understood largely to mean 'de-Stalinisation', that is the removal of specific features of the social order, but towards the end of the period it began to be taken to mean 'freedom and justice and the influence of society on government' (Marody et al. 1981). In the second place, this was a period during which society, or certain social groups, made three attempts to change the existing social order so that it would be better adapted to the values

17. Throughout the paper my interest lies with the society 'side'. The authorities 'side' will only appear when it is indispensable for understanding the collective actions of society. Obviously, a full development of the theoretical scheme suggested here would require a consideration of the actions, values and interests of both sides of the rulers–ruled relation.

18. Strzelecki (1984) has pointed to national reconstruction as value which formed the basis for cooperation with the authorities for people who it may be surmised had value systems fundamentally different from the value system declared by the authorities at that time.

19. This has been noted by Morawski (1980), who has written that 'the strategy of forced industrialisation' which in the approach adopted here may be regarded as an A value behind the authorities' decisions to change the social order, was realised with the consent of society, which saw it as an opportunity for achieving its own aspirations.

137

making up the collective sense. Although the 1970 attempt seemed to have been successful, the social order was not in fact disturbed in any fundamental way.

However, the events at the outset of the eighteen months between 1980 and 1981 did represent a real change in this order (Sulek 1984). The collective sense which formed the basis of the consensus remained the same in principle as throughout the previous period, except for the evolution of the concept of democratisation which I mentioned earlier.

The next change in the social order came on 13 December 1981, one which was introduced by force. After a short bargaining period a new collective sense matured. I shall deal with the period heralded by this change in the rest of the paper. However, I shall begin with a few remarks on the historical approach to matters relating to the collective sense.

Firstly, I have completely omitted the question of the form which successive social orders took. This is a subject which has often been addressed by Polish sociologists, and even a perfunctory consideration of the ideas which have been put forward in this connection is beyond the scope of this paper. It is worth noting, however, that the successive 'editions' of this social order did not totally negate the editions which preceded them. I share Rychard's view when he writes that 'each successive stage of development was characterised not so much by a rejection of elements of the previous stage as by the "addition" of new elements alongside the weakening of older ones' (1983: 49).[20] Thus the order which exists at present has inherited many elements from earlier periods.

Secondly, although the social order is always constructed on the basis of the actions of both the authorities and society, each side seems to control a different component in this order. For the authorities this is the institutional order and for society, the normative order. This may be tied in with the specific circumstances surrounding the genesis of the political system functioning in Poland (Narojek 1984; Rychard 1983).

Thirdly, although I use the general terms 'society' or 'the majority of society', I would like to emphasise that in each of the historical periods distinguished above, different groups were involved in the support of the authorities. In other words, different

20. Rychard accepts a similar chronology. He gives a more detailed description of the social orders corresponding to the three periods distinguished here.

social groups remained outside the scope of the negotiated consensus. These groups play an essential role in the theoretical schema presented here, for they are 'carriers' of values which, if they come to be espoused by the majority of society, may become elements of the collective senses negotiated in subsequent periods.[21]

I am aware that this schematic treatment of forty years of Polish history is open to criticism. However, my main concern is to illustrate rather abstract comments concerning the concept of the collective sense by showing how the concept may be applied. It is not the aim of this chapter to present an historical analysis. Its main interest lies in the connection between values, particularly those indicating the present level of acceptance of a social and political system, and social actions. I shall attempt to elucidate this connection by using the concept of the collective sense.

The Value System and Institutional Order in Polish Society

In the introduction I stated that the social and political picture of Poland in the mid-1980s which emerges from sociological studies and observation can be said to have two defining characteristics: (a) there is a rejection of the social and political system in the symbolic sphere, that is in the sphere of attitudes and values, and (b) there is an active or passive acceptance of the system in the sphere of action. In order to account for this apparent psychological contradiction, it is necessary to begin with a more detailed description of the system of values and needs which exists in Polish society, for on the one hand this system generates lack of acceptance of the political and social system, and on the other it channels human actions.

The Values and Needs of Polish Society

We shall not delve into the debates in the social sciences which surround the concept of a 'value' but take the term to mean a desired state of social reality connected with the idea of the 'good society'. The term 'need' will be taken to mean a desired state connected to an individuals notions of a 'worthwhile life'. According to this understanding, values and needs delimit the realm of

---

21. In this connection see Szawiel (1982). To the examples of ethos groups given by the author, such as Catholics, the democratic opposition and counter-culture groups, I would add the 'other side', that is the 'carriers' of 'totalitarian' values.

basic interests in society.

The system of values which are held in Polish society has often been subject to investigation. On the basis of these studies it emerges that this value system has been stable for some time. It consists of equality of opportunity, freedom of speech, democracy in the sense of the real influence of citizens on the government of the state, justice, truth, respect for human dignity, and prosperity or economic efficiency as a condition of this prosperity (Marody et al. 1981; S. Nowak 1979; S. Nowak and Lindenberg 1984). If it is possible to speak of change in or after August 1980, it would mainly consist of the decisiveness with which respondents currently make value choices.[22] To put this another way, the picture of what is the 'good society' is a clearer one and therefore less subject, if at all, to efforts at persuasion. The sphere of values has become a sphere of undebatable and obvious choices.

As far as the sphere of individual *needs* is concerned, it would seem useful to distinguish two general groups which have emerged in the studies. The first of these comprises material needs whose satisfaction guarantees a 'decent' standard of living. What constitutes this decent standard of living obviously differs according to social group. However, we can distinguish three basic conditions which must be met for the social consciousness of a 'normal' level of satisfaction of these needs:

(1) A wage level which allows the relatively problem-free satisfaction of material needs such as food, clothing and so on, and which affords the opportunity to save and buy at some foreseeable point in the future such non-luxury items as a refrigerator, washing-machine, television set and so on.[23]

(2) Accessibility of material goods, that is an adequate supply to the market.

(3) Having a flat.

These three conditions of social consciousness form the threshold below which one can talk of deprivation and above which there is an area of consumer choice related to material needs.

22. In 1983 the number of positive and negative features of the system which received 50 per cent of choices was greater than in 1978 (Nowak and Lindenberg 1984).

23. The concept of a 'norm' has obviously been reconstructed here on the basis of studies of social consciousness, and so from the point of view of economics the division of goods may seem to lack objective criteria here. Since both the concept of

The second group are psychological needs which form the existential dimension of life and whose satisfaction determines the 'psychological well-being' of an individual's existence. Those most frequently mentioned in surveys are:

(1) Dignity. This is primarily understood as the need for respect which respondents expect from others, both in direct contact with others as well as in the more depersonalised authorities–society relation — or in their less private roles of citizens of People's Poland.

(2) Freedom of speech, understood first and foremost as the individual's need to express his or her views without feeling threatened. This manifests itself, among other things, in rating truth highly among social values.

(3) Autonomy. This need manifests itself for the most part in the extremely negative attitude expressed towards those actions of the authorities which in the opinion of respondents represent an attempt to manipulate the actions and attitudes of society. This need may take two forms: the need for individual autonomy or the need for social autonomy. Both are connected to the question of collective action.

(4) A meaning in life. This has both an everyday and a more metaphysical dimension. In its everyday dimension it manifests itself as the desire to see social life as being efficiently organised, where actions are well articulated with each other and serve the realisation of some goal. That is to say, there is a desire that the life in which the individual participates be shaped in accordance with common sense. In its metaphysical dimension this need expresses itself as the desire for faith in something or someone, a faith which lends suprapersonal purpose and meaning to the life of the individual.

This group of needs, which we shall term 'existential needs' has two basic features. In the first place, these needs have numerous interconnections. For example, the need for dignity is closely connected to truth, which is the axiological basis for the need for freedom of speech; meaning in life is created through satisfying the needs for autonomy and dignity and so on. Secondly, these are

---

deprivation and that of satisfaction are ones which appeal to subjective experience (except for borderline cases), it would also seem reasonable to refer to subjective criteria in the sphere of material goods.

needs which are largely met through collective and not individual action, if only because the cooperation of other people is required in this, as is a particular form of social relations and institutional order.

Regardless of the distinction drawn here between material and existential needs, these needs should be treated together, since only in conjunction do they make up a 'worthwhile' life in social consciousness (Marody et al. 1981).

The link between the sphere of values and the sphere of needs in social consciousness also requires brief commentary. Social values may be autotelic in that the 'good society' which they define is viewed as a desired goal and valuable *in and of itself*. In Polish society, however, it is more usual that these values be treated *instrumentally* in relation to both material and existential needs. The values described above determine the kind of social order which in social consciousness is a necessary condition for the full satisfaction of individual needs and which thus constitutes the good society. This kind of connection anchors opinions concerning the current social and political order to the sphere of individual needs thereby linking concrete individual interests to abstract social interests.

Institutional Conditions of Action

We have already referred to the general lack of confidence in the highest institutions of the state. To the data quoted earlier we might add that only 22.4 per cent of respondents thought that the state administration was 'good' or 'very good', 56.5 per cent thought that it was inadequate or bad, while some 68.4 per cent thought that the number of officials employed in the state administration was too large.[24] There was also a widespread conviction among respondents that their influence on what happens at work and in society as a whole was small. In the case of influence in the workplace, the average opinion oscillated around 'inadequate', that is between 2.11 and 1.94 on a scale of 1 to 5. In the case of influence on social life, the average opinion varied between 1.83 and 1.55.[25] The statement 'everyone has an influence on the election of the authorities' was rejected by 56.3 per cent of respondents.[26] It is also characteristic that in responses to the question as to who should be able to put

24. CBOS data, August 1983; national sample (N=1,500).
25. See p. 130, n. 3.
26. Study in 1984 by Janicka, Koralewicz-Zębik, Mach, Skotnicka-Illiasiewicz and Wnuk-Lipiński; national sample (N=2,335).

forward candidates for workers' councils, most support was given to options outside current electoral law. Of those replying, 72.6 per cent said that not only PRON (see p. 19, n. 14) but other groups such as tenants' associations and housing cooperative committees should also have this right; 57.4 per cent said that in addition to organisations and associations, sufficiently large groups of voters should also be able to put forward candidates.[27]

It is therefore possible to say that respondents see the institutional order as being ineffective for meeting the needs of society. Nor does it contribute to the realisation of basic values associated with the concept of the 'good society' since the respondents largely attribute characteristics to it which they view as undesirable. If we accept Lipset's (1959) statement that one condition for the stability of a system is confidence (legitimation) and belief in the effectiveness of the institutions of social life, then we have to say that current Polish institutions are held in low regard on both counts. We should therefore be dealing with attempts to change the social order. Since such a conclusion would clearly be out of line with reality, we shall merely say that the institutional order is judged by respondents to be inadequate for the task of meeting the needs and realising the values of Polish society. This finds general expression *inter alia* in the fact that 83.6 per cent of respondents believe that the difficulties which people are currently experiencing are 'very painful' or 'rather painful'.[28]

This negative appraisal of the institutional order is not only important because it points to the subjectively felt impossibility of satisfying needs or observing the values which are espoused within this social order. It is also important because it is accompanied by a sense of humiliation ('We, a great and heroic nation and such beggars'). This increases the aversion felt towards those in power, for it was they who established the institutional order within which daily life runs its course; it also deepens the split between the concepts of society and state which are taken to designate two *separate entities* (S. Nowak 1979).

The Present Collective Sense

The basic split which has been ascertained between society's values

27. CBOS data, February 1984; national sample (N=1,497).
28. CBOS data, July 1984; workers (N=2,041).

and needs and the extent to which their realisation is subjectively felt to be possible within the existing institutional order confronts the researcher with the question as to how this split comes to be tolerated by society. According to the theoretical assumptions which were made above, there are two possible answers to this question. First, the stability of the present order can be guaranteed by force. However, this answer seems rather unrealistic. We must therefore search for another explanation among the values which can form the basis of social consensus. In other words, we have had to identify what these values currently are.

The consensus which now exists between society and those in power was formed in the name of 'social peace' and 'welfare security', and these two values make up the current collective sense. These two aspects of social life acquired special importance in the period immediately preceding martial law, and retain their significance to the present day.

As a desired value, 'social peace' increased in importance for a large section of society because of the growing anxiety towards the end of 1981, which reached a climax with the introduction of martial law and persisted as a result of government propaganda efforts. This high anxiety level would seem to have its source in three kinds of fears:

(1) Fear of war, including civil war and invasion.
(2) Fear of the growing anarchy of social life.
(3) Fear associated with the perception of many social actions as 'illegal' or punishable.

These three types of fear are clearly manifested in sociological studies. For example, 85.5 per cent of respondents agreed with the excerpt from one of Jaruzelski's speeches which stated that the Poles 'are celebrating [their] fortieth anniversary in a tense and dangerous international situation', although only 12.2 per cent were of the opinion that Jaruzelski's speeches were 'in accordance with what [they] think'.[29] From other studies it emerges that Polish society has a negative view of all forms of social protest which involve a disruption of public order.[30] In yet other surveys, 16.8 per cent of respondents admitted that they would vote out of fear in the

---

29. CBOS data, July 1984; sample of urban population in twelve cities (N=516).
30. Adamski, Białecki et al. (1981); nationwide sample.

elections to the people's councils,[31] 22.4 per cent thought that not voting would expose them to unpleasantness from the authorities,[32] and of 45 per cent of respondents who believed that the majority of citizens obeyed authority, 79 per cent accepted the view that the reason for this subordination was the fact that the authorities could punish disobedience.[33]

The argument that 'social peace' is now an important value for Polish society is also supported by more direct data. For example, in one survey respondents were asked to complete unfinished sentences. Of the seventy-one persons who completed the sentence 'For us the most important thing is . . .', seventeen wrote 'peace and quiet', thirteen wrote 'peace and work' while four wrote 'agreement in the country'. In 1984, 55.7 per cent of respondents approved of the introduction of martial law (definitely or on the whole), and this percentage has been rising. In addition 11.7 per cent thought that it was in the interest of society only, 32.8 per cent that it was in the interest only of those in power, and 41.3 per cent that it was in the interests of both society and those in power.[34] In the same study, of the 45 per cent of respondents who believed that the majority of citizens obey authority, 78.5 per cent accepted the view that 'people submit to authority since this makes it easier for them to live and see to different matters'. This is evidence of the passive acceptance of the social and political system and shows the instrumentality of this acceptance. We shall return to this question later.

As a desired quality of social life, 'welfare security' gained importance during the period preceding the introduction of martial law as a result of an increasing feeling of helplessness. Strictly speaking, we should say that during this period the sense of helplessness which was associated with the experience of social conflict overlapped with two deeper features of Polish social consciousness, that is the idea of the welfare state which was linked to the concept of socialism, and an attitude of 'acquired helplessness'.

As far as the first of these two features is concerned, despite the fact that support for 'real socialism' is rather weak, 'theoretical socialism' still enjoys considerable support among respondents.[35] In many surveys the difference in the percentage of supporting re-

31. See p. 142, n. 26.
32. CBOS data, May 1984; national sample (N=1,486).
33. See p. 131, n. 5.
34. Ibid.
35. I use these abbreviations to stand for two questions which often occur in Polish sociological studies: (a) 'Would you wish the world to move in the direction

sponses approaches 40 points. This seems to have its origins in the positive features which are attributed to socialism as a theoretical system, particularly when it is compared with capitalism. For example, 50 per cent of respondents believe that there is more injustice and exploitation under capitalism than under socialism, while 27 per cent reject this view. While 46 per cent believe that socialism is more progressive than capitalism, 26 per cent reject this view, and 70 per cent believe that socialism is better as far as assuring people work and a secure future.[36]

It seems that these views are often transposed from 'theoretical' to 'real' socialism, especially since the latter for all its inefficiency still retains the advantage in social conciousness over capitalism that it is seen as assuring work and, by the same token, the future. This sense of greater security, even if it has largely been constructed through propaganda, is reinforced by the habits and attitudes which are formed in the course of the individual's daily experience.

The Polish citizen is not afraid of losing his or her job. If one fears anything it is that one will have to change jobs *oneself*, usually because of bad relationships at one's present place of work. The origins of this fear are to be found in the attitude of 'learned helplessness' (Seligman 1975). In psychology this concept refers to an attitude which forms as a result of repeated participation in situations over which the individual has no control. This learned helplessness is then transposed to other situations, making the individual incapable of actions which require initiative.

The long experience of a life organised by the authorities has encouraged people to shift responsibility for the shape of their lives to those authorities. It has also meant that they have lost the capacity for actively shaping their own lives, on the level of society, but not on the level of private life.[37] The research workers who complain that their institution did not *give* them a research topic, and workers who say that work should be organised so that a person shouldn't *have to* bodge the job, are clear examples of this.

---

of the form of socialism which exists in Poland?' (real socialism) and (b) 'Would you wish the world to move in the direction of some form of socialism?' (theoretical socialism).

36. See p. 131, n. 5.

37. In Polish conditions the attitude of acquired helplessness seems to have a situational character; that is, to use Narojek's (1984) words, it is connected with 'the nationalisation of initiatives for action in collective life'. In those areas of social life and at those time when the authorities allow private or non-state initiatives in action — usually as a result of pressure — the attitude of acquired helplessness disappears.

This learned helplessness is reinforced by fear of responsibility. Fear is generated by the absence of clearly articulated criteria for this responsibility on the one hand, and on the other by the continual amendments to the instructions issued by the authorities for the regulation of the institutional order. So in a situation where one suspects the existence of learned helplessness among a considerable section of society, the absence of unemployment and the lack of responsibility for one's own fate become important values. Their importance was heightened during the pre-martial law period due to the social conflict between the authorities and Solidarity, to which no solution could be envisaged. An increasing number of people began to find social reality incomprehensible, and they had little idea of how to behave in this reality. A clear expression of this helplessness was the increase in 'can't say' responses which emerged in sociological surveys between 1980 and 1981 (Adamski, Beskid et al. 1982). More recent data indicates that this is a continuing trend. In many studies the percentage of 'optimists' — those who believe in the possibility of rapid (within two years) or slower (between ten and fifteen years) emergence from the crisis, oscillates around 30 per cent. For the majority of respondents the future appears either as an unknown, or a continuation or decline of an already difficult situation. Since the majority of respondents see *effective* measures for overcoming the crisis as involving a reform of the political system, which in turn they view as unlikely to take place, the result is an intensification of the sense of helplessness, and a confinement to short-term planning. For example, 27 per cent of students surveyed in one study said they were unable to say what the country would be like five years hence, while 43 per cent did not or could not say what their own position would be five years hence.[38]

This confinement to short-term planning relates not only to the private life of individuals but also to public life. There are studies which show that enterprise management teams usually only plan three months ahead; the longest planning period is to the end of the year. In both public and private life people concentrate on the problems which arise from daily events and look for extemporaneous solutions, avoiding the longer-term implications of this.

The growing sense of anxiety and helplessness has led in many cases to the belief that any social order at all is better than none. For where there is no order, no rules of individual behaviour can be

38. See p. 130, n. 2.

formulated. Since the slogans of 'social peace' and 'welfare security' also created a convenient point from which the authorities could begin to construct a social order which would maximise the chances of realising A values and A needs, they were able to form the basis for the negotiation of the subsequent social consensus.[39]

The Collective Sense and Action

The current social consensus has two more general features which are worth mentioning because of their influence on current social action. Firstly, as we have defined it, the collective sense is in fact an 'anti-sense' since, because of its defensive and passive qualities, it cannot channel social effort. The most it can do is to keep members of society from undertaking certain collective actions. This means that by accepting 'social peace' and 'welfare security' as the basis of consensus society at least temporarily relinquishes the chance of creating a unifying principle to guide its actions. In other words, society has in a certain sense 'dissolved' and the social principle of unification has been replaced by a political principle. However, the complete absorption of society by the state can only take place, it would seem, when the state is a totalitarian one (Rychard 1983; Buber 1983). Polish social consciousness is far from being able to form the basis for the construction of such a state.

On the other hand, one can say that the social function of such values as 'social peace' and 'welfare security' in essence represent the defence of what members of society have already got. This is supported by empirical data which show that the main area of individual action is 'defence against becoming *declassé*'. In other words, Polish society has not reconciled itself to the need for lowering its standard of living, which has been the direct effect of economic crisis. Instead, it is actively attempting to bolster the level of consumption which it had previously attained. This defence takes place at the cost of other possible areas of action. This conclusion is warranted by an analysis of changes which have taken place in individual time-budgets between 1976 and 1982. The author of a study comparing these time-budgets has written:

> the time reserves which have been gained by persons employed in the
> state economy both as a result of shortening working hours and cutting

39. See data from the end of 1981 (in Jasiewicz's 1982 study) which indicate growing support in various social groups for the 'Party of law and order'.

down on free time and the time spent on meeting physiological needs has been almost totally taken up by domestic chores. . . . When faced with crisis, people have directed all their activities to meeting material needs and bringing up the children, at the cost even of such basic needs as sleep (Milic-Czerniak 1985).

People do this in several ways. First and foremost they switch to a form of 'do-it-yourself' whereby family members provide many of the services and even produce many of the articles which were formerly purchased on the market. Secondly, and this applies primarily to women, paid employment is substituted for by domestic labour, either through giving up paid employment completely (and going on childcare leave), or through giving up work which provided extra income, such as overtime or moonlighting. The ability to use one's time flexibly is in many cases a more effective way of safeguarding one's level of consumption than is increased income, whose purchasing power has been reduced by inflation. Thirdly, many people both of pre-productive age (i.e. schoolchildren and students) or of post-productive age (i.e. old-age pensioners) have entered the labour market: 'The percentage of people in the first category who are making extra money is almost twice as high as it was in 1976, while in the second category it has increased fourfold' (Milic-Czerniak 1985). In the case of those employed in the private sector, especially farmers, the consumption level is safeguarded by spending more time at work.

Regardless of whether it is extra work at home or at the workplace which is involved, all of the time which can be made available by making 'cuts' in other areas is absorbed. This withdrawal from other areas of activity, mainly from those which might disturb the 'social peace' should in our terms be viewed as the effect of a compromise between the authorities and society. According to this compromise the adherence of both sides to the collective sense guarantees both sides maximum realisation under the existing conditions of the other values and aspirations which they have. Hence one may assume that the values which make up the collective sense will begin to lose their importance for society when they cease to perform these safeguarding functions.[40] For these reasons the present consensus must be regarded as a temporary one, that is one which may be questioned in the immediate future either by society

---

40. That they cannot perform them is known to some extent from economic forecasts.

or by the authorities.

The second important feature of the current social consensus is the fact that in practice all the desires and aspirations of individuals which are important for Polish society remain outside the negotiated collective sense. This lack of consistency between the values which make up the collective sense and the desires and aspirations which form the basis of individual needs can be clearly seen in the appraisal made of the institutional order which determines the realisation of both. Respondents see this order as one which does not create a way of meeting needs which would be consistent with the notions of a 'worthwhile life' which form the threshold of social frustration.

We are dealing then with a situation in which the institutional order, although it is not accepted, cannot be questioned by society, since it serves at least in theory to realise the negotiated collective sense. On the other hand, even the minimum satisfaction of individual needs requires participation in a social life whose institutions are determined by this order. These two opposing tendencies lead to a phenomenon in the sphere of action which I will term the 'reprivatisation of social life'. By reprivatisation I mean a change in the way individual needs are satisfied where broadly speaking there is a withdrawal from public life, the framework of which is determined by the officially established institutional order, or there is an infringement of this order which does not alter its fundamental form. More specifically, the phenomenon involves the prevalence of a particular adjustment strategy in the sphere of action. This is a traditional strategy since it occurred in earlier periods of Poland's postwar history, although less intensely than at present. The basis of the strategy is the acceptance of the existing institutional order as a 'necessary evil' and the attempt to capitalise on the opportunities which are unintentionally created by this order. The strategy has an individual and collective version:

(a) *The individual version.* The individual strategy is characterised firstly by the suspension of matters of principle and concentration on the pragmatic aspect of action. Secondly, it means participation in the so-called second economy in the case of material needs. This second economy refers to economic activities which are not registered and hence are exempt from taxation. This includes such activities as illegal private work during hours of employment, speculative activity, street vending, income from the sale of produce from private allotments, income from undeclared services performed in private workshops, and so on. According to the estimates of some economists, this second economy accounts for from 10.2 to 12.1 per cent of personal incomes (Bednarski 1984). Both participation in the second economy and changes in time-budgets may be regarded as signs of a more general tendency to search for ways of coping with reality outside the officially established institutional order. Thirdly, in the case of existential needs there is a shift from the public to the private sphere of life. The family and close friends have become the main arena for the satisfaction of existential needs, although they are to some extent a substitute in view of the connection these needs have with public life. The meaning of life is sought in bringing up one's children, the satisfaction of the need for respect and autonomy in actions taken to prevent downward social mobility, and the satisfaction of the need for freedom of speech in private discussions. For many people religious participation seems to play a similar role, for many studies of social consciousness indicate its essentially private nature. The shift seems to be even broader than this, however, and also manifests itself in a changed attitude to paid employment. For example, informal norms and principles are transposed to formal organisations — for instance, the belief that a clerk has to 'like' me in order to arrange my business (and the behaviour patterns associated with this belief), the place of employment is regarded as an extension of one's domestic workplace, and finally one's salary may come to be regarded as a benefit payment which is due merely for turning up at work; the latter is associated with a transfer of energy to areas of activity outside employment.

The individual adjustment strategy is accompanied by two phenomena. One is the attractiveness of options which place the individual outside or alongside the system — for example, working for a Polonia firm,[41] going on childcare leave or going abroad for a period. Such choices are not purely economically motivated but are also linked to a whole range of existential needs, particularly among the intelligentsia. The other is the improved adaptation of specific norms of behaviour to the dominant institutional order. For example, on a general level 57.4 per cent of respondents disapprove of those who shirk work; no-one regards this as normal. On the other

41. Private firms set up by foreigners of Polish extraction, where wages are generally higher than in the state sector.

hand, on the level of specifics only 31 per cent disapprove of illegal private work during hours of employment while 16 per cent regard it as normal. The arrangement of private business during working hours is disapproved of by 22.4 per cent of respondents, while 24.5 per cent regard it as normal.[42]

The individual adjustment strategy is supported by the rather common belief that 'the authorities have very little influence on what people like me actually do'. This view was expressed by 53.6 per cent of respondents.[43] This belief is the psychological basis for 'the acceptance of the unacceptable'. In other words, a belief in freedom of action in the individual sphere compensates for the frustration arising from the impossibility of action in the social sphere. This is expressed, among other things, in the appearance of a new category of social differentiation in questionaire responses. In addition to the traditional categories which describe those who are better or worse off, such as private entrepreneurs, pensioners and so on, respondents also mention those who are 'resourceful' and 'not resourceful'.[44] This supports the view that individual effort is seen as an effective way of dealing with social reality.

The objective effectiveness of individual adjustment strategies seems to be limited both quantitatively, for example with regard to the possibilities for going 'outside the system', and from the point of view of time (as with economic forecasts). This is not to say that they are ineffective from the subjective point of view. This is because by its very nature the adjustment strategy has no natural checks, since a modification of means entails a modification of the goals these means were meant to safeguard. For this reason it is to be expected that an individual adjustment strategy will lead to 'slippage' and an ever-decreasing standard of living.

(b) The collective version. The collective adjustment strategy mainly consists of taking advantage of the opportunities which have been unintentionally created by the institutional order, for the realisation of group interests. The group and hence also the collective aspect of these strategies appear at the level of the enterprise. Adjustment strategies of this type are characterised by efforts to increase group earnings. They are based on the rationality of existing regulations and not the rationality of the economy as a whole. Actions of this

---

42. CBOS data, September 1983; sample of urban population (N=967).
43. See p. 131, n. 5.
44. Ibid.

type have been adequately described both by economists and organisational sociologists, and so I shall not deal with them here.

The strike represents a particular collective adjustment strategy adopted after 13 December 1981. As a form of protest at enterprise level, the strike figured in fifth place in a list of actions in which respondents said they themselves would participate, after speaking at a meeting of the workers' self-governing body, complaining to the management, drawing up a joint letter to the authorities and appealing to the labour unions. The strike appears in first place among those forms of actions where those against begin to outweigh those for. However it occupies third place when the same actions are evaluated from the point of view of effectiveness.[45] From the fragmentary data which we have concerning current strikes, we may conclude that fear of this form of protest is overcome when real and not symbolic goals are involved. Since bargaining usually concerns wages and not the shortcomings of the management system (i.e. it is the interests of a particular social group and not the institutional order which is at stake as it was in and after August 1980), the strike may be viewed as part of a collective adjustment strategy.

Three more general remarks remain to be made concerning the reprivatisation of social life. Firstly, in both versions of the adjustment strategy, although the institutional order is not violated, the normative order is modified. Rules of behaviour are introduced as *fait accompli* into the actual social order which can begin to split it from the inside.

Secondly, the stabilising function of both adjustment strategies is dependent on their effectiveness, that is on the extent to which they really help to meet individual needs. There are two external checks on these strategies: both versions of the adjustment strategy depend on possibilities which have been unintentionally created by the authorities. These can be withdrawn at any moment by legislation. In addition, in the long term these strategies will lead to a disintegration rather than change of the existing social order.

Thirdly and finally, newspaper articles and sociological reports have often noted a high level of frustration of social needs and values in recent years. They have drawn the conclusion that the consequence of this frustration is apathy — and an increase in social pathology, but I shall not go into that problem here. In the light of

45. Study by Ziółkowski in 1984; workers (N=130).

the present analysis, I do not believe that apathy can be attributed to Polish society, despite the high level of frustration which does exist. Rather, there is a high level of activity, but this activity takes place in the private domain. It would also be difficult to describe social attitudes to the public domain as apathetic. Rather, there is a wait-and-see attitude and a suspension of activity.

This wait-and-see approach is seen in an additional strategy for coping with reality which emerges in sociological studies. It is manifested in the *transformation strategy* which represents an attempt to influence the shape of social life by enforcing the legal framework of existing institutions, even though the authorities may treat these laws as a mere façade. Perhaps the term 'strategy' is a misnomer here, since what we are talking about are isolated attempts rather than consciously organised action to reconstruct the social and political system. However, it is important to indicate the existence of such efforts, since in my opinion the transformation strategy is the most interesting way of coping with social reality. The most spectacular example of this strategy was the challenge in court of the election results in several electoral constituencies. The action which has had the broadest scale has been the use of the labour courts as an instrument for exacting workers' rights, particularly in the period immediately following martial law.

These are examples of individual actions, however. The adoption of the transformation strategy by institutionally organised groups would be more significant for the shape of social life. For this reason it is worth noting the activities of workers' self-governing bodies, since it is they who are the most frequent vehicles of the transformation strategy, although in absolute terms even this does not happen often. The self-governing bodies are used because they represent the only institution whose roots are in the pre-martial law period and whose possibilities were not exhausted at that time.

The results of studies of social consciousness, particularly among workers in large industrial enterprises, justify our view of self-governing bodies as a vehicle for influencing the shape of social life. For example, when asked about the powers of self-governing bodies, 66.1 per cent of respondents were of the opinion that they should make the decisions relating to all the most important issues affecting the enterprise. When asked about the division of authority between enterprise director and the self-governing body, 56.2 per cent of respondents thought that the self-governing body and the enterprise director should form a collective management, while 26.5

per cent went even further and thought that the self-governing body should be the one to decide, while the enterprise director should execute its decisions. Finally, 64.4 per cent of respondents believed that the manager should be recruited by open competition and should be appointed by and be accountable to the self governing body.[46]

It should be emphasised that so far the self-governing body has mainly been seen as an institution which represents the social interests of an enterprise's *workforce* (50.9 per cent of respondents held this view). It could therefore be included among collective adjustment strategies, were it not for the fact that the safeguarding of their interests is seen as *influencing* rather than *taking advantage of* the existing shape of social life. This is illustrated by the fact that certain self-governing bodies are attempting to enforce their rights in court and more indirectly by the fact that the opinions that 'self-governing bodies should only exist at enterprise level' and 'workers' self-governing bodies should have their own Seym representation' receive the same amount of support, with 42.6 per cent of respondents concurring in each case. It is worth adding that 24 per cent of respondents supported the view that a self-governing body should represent the interests of society as a whole. This is also support for the thesis that at least part of society sees this institution as a vehicle for influencing the shape of social life.[47]

The transformation strategy is not a fully developed approach but rather represents the beginnings of new forms of action. There is, however, a broader psychological background to it. When asked whether PRON (see p. 19, n. 14) and the new trade unions merit confidence, respondents answered 'can't say' in 32.5 per cent and 39.9 per cent of cases, respectively. With other institutions such a response was given in roughly 15 per cent of cases.[48] This wait-and-see approach to the new social institutions emerges even more clearly in the fact that 47.5 per cent of respondents replied 'can't say' when asked whether new trade unions were independent and self-governing; among persons who were not members of the new unions, 55.2 per cent gave the same response.[49]

The wait-and-see approach is reinforced further by an awareness,

46. Department of Sociological Studies, IOMP, September 1984; workers (N=210).
47. Ibid.
48. See p. 131, n. 5.
49. CBOS data, November 1983; workers (N=2,136).

at least in some social groups, of the limited objective effectiveness of individual adjustment strategies and the perceived inadequacy, again among certain groups, of substitutes for the satisfaction of existential needs, especially the need for autonomy.

The effectiveness of the transformation strategy depends on two main factors: firstly, society's legal awareness, which is regarded as being rather low and, secondly, the nature of legislation, which allows to a greater or lesser extent for groups or individuals to influence the shape of social life. This latter factor means that the scope of freedom of social action in the transformation strategy depends largely on the measures taken by the authorities. The kind of social life which now exists in Poland depends both on the official institutional order and the strategies for action which we have described above.

The Distribution of Social Forces

In the concluding section of this paper we shall attempt to draw up a provisional classification of the social forces which exist in Poland at the present time. I am only too aware of how deceptive estimates based on the results of sociological investigations can be. However, it would be useful to put forward a classification which is based not only on social and demographic criteria, but which also makes reference to social consciousness. This classification contains at least five sub-groups:

(1) The 'adherents to socialism': persons who accept the current social and political system on the basis of principle. This is not tantamount to accepting Marxist ideology *in toto*, hence the inverted commas. They are convinced that this system realises or at least makes possible the eventual realisation of the basic social values which they espouse. This group is estimated to constitute about 12 per cent of society as a whole. People in this category tend to have a lower level of education, be older, belong to the Party or to have careers connected with the Party, propaganda, the trade unions or the military apparatus.

(2) The state-builders: persons who accept the current social and political system for pragmatic reasons. The most important of these is a belief that for *raisons d'état* certain basic features

156

of Poland's social and political system should be retained, and the link between a person's own career with the institutional order created by the authorities. This group constitutes about 15 per cent of society as a whole, and tends to contain those in senior management, those with higher education, Party members and trade union members.

(3) The 'opposition': persons who reject the present social and political system not only in the symbolic sphere but also to a greater or lesser extent in the sphere of action — this is not the same as active opposition, hence the inverted commas. They do this for reasons of principle, since they believe that the present system violates the basic values which they espouse. Some studies estimate that this group forms 7 per cent of Polish society. The people in this category tend to have higher education, are more likely to be skilled workers and to have been active during the Solidarity period.

(4) 'Opposition' sympathisers: persons who do not accept the current social and political system mainly on pragmatic grounds. That is to say, the present system does not give them the chance to satisfy individual needs, either material or existential. Although their rejection is largely confined to the symbolic sphere making their behaviour similar to those in the next group, they nevertheless sometimes undertake actions which, although within the law, are at least by intention inconsistent with the realised institutional order, for example failure to vote in elections. This group is estimated to form between 18 and 20 per cent of society. The people in this group tend to be young, have an education beyond elementary level and to be white-collar or skilled workers.

(5) 'The rest': these persons reject the social and political system on a symbolic level; they adopt an adjustment strategy on the level of action and passively accept the institutional order in the name of the values which constitute the collective sense. This category represents between 46 and 48 per cent of society. Within this group it is possible to distinguish a sub-group referred to in sociological studies as the 'silent minority' (Adamski, Beskid et al. 1982). This sub-group accounts for about 15 per cent of society and is marked by a kind of intellectual helplessness on socio-political matters. This is evidenced by the frequency of such responses as 'can't say' or 'I have no opinion' in surveys. These are people who,

because of their lack of clearly defined views, will latch onto every majority. Such persons tend to be older, have a low level of education and to be unskilled workers or have no trade.

Groups 1 and 2 provide social support for the government. They consist of people who either believe in the possibility of realising the 'principles' embodied in the system, or in the possibility of utilising the system to safeguard certain values, for example the existence of the Polish state, or to satisfy certain needs. Groups 3 and 4 provide the social support for the opposition in a wide sense. They include persons who might be summed up as having no illusions with respect to the socio-political system in which they have to live, although this attitude, it should be remembered, has varying effects with regard to action. These two more general categories are of about the same size; for this reason the way the social situation develops depends on group 5. People's line of action is determined in this case by an unstable equilibrium between a sense of anxiety on the one hand and a sense of threat to the satisfaction of material needs on the other. Which of these prevails in social consciousness will determine the direction of collective action.

The social trends which I have outlined in this chapter apply with varying strength to all groups. At the present time it seems that members of groups 3 and 4 will remain outside the negotiated consensus. They are also the main carriers of the values which define the desired social order, and it is they who feel most strongly the frustration caused by the impossibility of meeting those needs which make up the 'worthwhile' life. In future negotiations between the government and society — if they take place at all, for there is always the possibility of having solutions imposed by force or that adjustment strategies will reign supreme — these values and needs will continue to define society's demands.

EDMUND WNUK-LIPIŃSKI

Social Dimorphism and its Implications

Polish scholars have recently become concerned with the external signs of a split in the social life of the country. Private and public worlds, the real world and that which is officially acknowledged, and the values, beliefs and attitudes associated with each, seem to have gone in quite different directions. The existence of this bifurcation has been confirmed by a recent reassessment of empirical data from the 1970s. According to this reassessment, what was 'remarkable in people's state of mind during the 1970s was the fact that a boundary was maintained between (a) a real and falsified image of reality and (b) what existed and what was supposed to exist. As a result attempts to manipulate people's consciousness had little effect' (Koralewicz-Zębik 1983b: 26). Elsewhere the same phenomenon has been analysed from a slightly different theoretical perspective (Wnuk-Lipiński 1982). Here it is argued that there is a major cleavage in Polish social life. That domain which is controlled by the authorities, the public domain, has its own system of values which does not operate outside this domain. The private domain, which refuses to submit to control, is governed by a different set of values. An individual thus has to orientate himself or herself towards one of two different sets of values, depending on whether he or she is dealing with the public or private world. I refer to this phenomenon as the 'dimorphism of values', and in what follows I shall develop this idea with reference to hypotheses suggested by recent events in Poland. I shall begin by defining the phenomenon and its preconditions more closely and go on to identify some of the more significant methodological implications of my theoretical position.

159

The Phenomenon and Its Preconditions

Why do people not say in public what they say in private? To put it
at its simplest, why do private opinions and behaviour usually differ
from those manifested in public? What are the reasons for this
duality in social life? What are its origins and why is it greater in
certain types of social order than in others?

A duality of social life has been observed in highly diverse
societies ranging from the primitive to the sophisticated and modern. One might therefore conclude that dimorphism is inherent in
all social life. This view would seem to be supported by symbolic
interactionist studies where an individual by defining his or her
situation enters into a specific game with his or her social environment, where people are classified as actors or audience, as being in
the background or in the limelight. This is the phenomenon Ossowski (1967a: 89) had in mind when he referred to 'weekday' and
'Sunday' values.

The conclusion is that some forms of social dimorphism are
probably a permanent feature of any human society. An individual
always lives according to his or her own genuine definitions of the
environment, but is also apt to interpret part of the environment in
ritualised terms which are imposed by a person's current social role.
The form of social dimorphism which interests me is systemic
rather than individual or even institutional and is characteristic of
certain societies.

Social dimorphism consists of the split of social life into two
relatively isolated domains, that is the public and the private. This
split can only be maintained under conditions of external coercion,
a statist economy where public life is subordinate to a single control
centre which has not been subject to democratic selection but which
has been imposed by some means or other. As a result, the centre
need not be orientated to the predominant value system in the
community but espouses and tries to impose a different, occasionally incompatible value system on this community.

This kind of split occurs both in small isolated total groups such
as prisons or military units, and in whole societies. Dimorphism on
the scale of an entire social system only appears possible in a
monocentric order. Ossowski has expressed this in the following
way:

The monocentric social order occurs in its purest form in a perfectly

disciplined military or bureaucratic organisation where there is a hierarchy of decision and control centres and where dilution of power is ruled
out in principle as a result of division of responsibility and strict subordination. Even where there is a margin for individual decision-taking, or
the interpretation of commands, higher authorities can always cancel
such decisions, or where the decision has already been implemented,
those responsible can be punished. Under these conditions decisions
taken on the authority of a particular position are tantamount to attempts
at guessing what will be approved by one's superiors. The habit of
obedience, which must become a universal virtue in this kind of social
system, can be extended in various ways. (Ossowski 1967b: 177)

The question thus arises as to what brings about the discrepancies
between the public and private domains. In the model social system
described here, the public domain is controlled by the centre in
three ways. The first of these is language, or more strictly, the
official semantic code in which communication takes place by
means of ritualised symbols. The second is law, or the subjection of
law to the control centre, which can thus almost arbitrarily make
any of its decisions legal. It is in this rather strange sense that no
action of the centre is ever illegal, for it is not action which stems
from the law but the law which follows from the actions of the
centre. According to this principle, any action which is independent
of the centre, not to mention those actions which are incompatible
with its expectations, can be held to be illegal, even in retrospect.
Under these circumstances the law is not a product of social
consensus which is based in a nation's culture and tradition but
rather an instrument for legalising whatever the centre chooses to
do. Finally, the third way in which the public domain is controlled
by the centre is through the direct enforcement of collective loyalty
by violent means, even if this is only apparent loyalty which persists
only as long as there is a threat of violence.

The power centre creates social institutions which are subordinate to it and which in the model case should fill out the whole
space of public social life. In practice, of course, the centre cannot
achieve this. For example, in Poland the independence of the
Church and the private farmers distort the model. The hierarchical
structure of social life is thus not fully achieved for there are at least
two relatively independent actors on the public scene.

From the point of view of what interests us here, the current
situation is sufficiently similar to that which existed before August
1980 for us to be able to speak of continuity rather than change.

Social dimorphism, which was significantly reduced during Solidarity's period of legal activity, has once more become an extremely widespread phenomenon and one whose contrasts are, if anything, even sharper than before.

The Preconditions of Social Dimorphism

In order to understand social dimorphism in Poland, one has to realise that in the aftermath of the Second World War the values of Western civilisation which had influenced Polish culture for over ten centuries came into conflict with an ideology permeated with Eastern values and an Asiatic system of public institutions. Two incompatible value systems therefore co-existed, one anchored in the ideology of the ruling stratum which dominated public life, and the other rooted in the nation's historical culture which has retreated to the private domain and to the level of small informal groups.

What then are the conditions which must be met for social dimorphism to come about at all? Experience shows that there are at least seven such preconditions:

(1) The ideology of the ruling group has to be culturally alien to that of the community which it governs.

(2) The culture of the community must be sufficiently vital for its traditional values to survive outside public institutions.

(3) The ruling group must be powerful or threatening enough to stay in power and to control the public stage.

(4) The socio-political system must be monocentric and statist, for only in this kind of system is the control of practically the whole of the public domain possible. In this kind of system the control of language — that is, the ability to create an official semantic code — is a substitute for the legitimisation of power. Control over the law allows for the legalisation, even in retrospect, of any decision the centre might make. Sufficient means of physical coercion ensures the stability of the whole system.

(5) New members of the ruling elite are not recruited on a meritocratic basis but according to political criteria. Becoming a member of the ruling class implies at least superficial acceptance of the values of the dominant ideology and a shift of loyalty to the values of the ruling group. This is what the

institution commonly known as *nomenklatura* is all about.

(6) The law does not provide for a changeover of power and is highly repressive with regard to any activity aimed at this kind of changeover. Since the ruling group is the sole legislator, the law need not be based on those values on which the rest of the national culture is founded, but rather protects the interests and objectives of the ruling group.

(7) The community recognises the duality of social life as a relatively permanent feature of social reality and can envisage no alternative to it.

Some of these conditions are familiar and have been discussed in the literature; others require comment. The socio-political system which was grafted onto Poland following the Second World War has never managed to break out of the vicious circle in which it found itself. The cautious reforms which were intermittently introduced at the top were held in check by the rank and file of the ruling class, who felt that even these timid reforms threatened their interests. More radical attempts at reform were suppressed by force because they would have led to an irrevocable loss of the system's monocentric identity. As the centre is well aware, the system cannot free itself from the trap whereby orthodox doctrine leads to economic deadlock and eventually to social disruption, while too far-reaching reforms might mean a loss of identity for the political system.

Doctrinal orthodoxy used to provide and probably continues to provide the frame of reference for intra-Party bargaining, and at the same time serves as a standard against which 'ideological distortions' are measured. The system of dogmas embodied in these standards has undergone modification, but this has not changed their content or created new values which might attract a larger section of the community. Directly and indirectly these dogmas continue to form the ideological ground on which the ruling class stands.

On the other hand, the foundations of Polish national culture have always been closely interwoven with Christianity. The baptism of Poland in 966 brought the country into European culture, and there it remains. Ancient tradition whereby moral norms are shaped by Christian ethics has become part of the national heritage. These norms have spread out from the strictly religious community to the broader cultural community. Given this background, the

163

grafting of culturally alien institutions onto Polish society could not but fail within any short historical timespan; the experience of over a hundred years of foreign domination in the public domain was still in the nation's memory. After the Second World War the traditional value system was transferred to the non-institutional area of the system of social relations. The only exception in this process has been in the case of the clerical institutions, which have managed to retain a real, albeit self-limited, independence. Whether they wish it or not, these institutions have been acting as a substitute axiological substratum for the values which were not embodied in any other public institution.

What was particularly alien in the new ideology was its perception of the individual. The traditional value system reinforced individualism while the new system was collectivist. In its more extreme forms it tended to reduce individuals to building blocks for the collective, depriving them of their own free will. In the traditional system individuals exercised their free will within the limits of Christian ethics which provided the axiological standards of self-realisation. If traced far enough back, this value system would probably be found to stem from the ethos of the nobility. According to the new system, however, the individual would find fulfilment in the life of the collective, in his or her usefulness to the broader community and by subordination to the group. Although this line of thought is present in populist or folk ethos, it has never gained a significant grip on the mind of the nation. The moral imperative is in the first place to obey the moral norms of one's culture and only secondly to obey the higher levels of the political hierarchy and thus conform to the group.

The individualistic elements in what I am here calling the traditional system used to be strongly linked to what is referred to as the dignity of the individual. In official ideology, too, this is emphasised, as in the much-quoted formula: 'In socialism the highest value is man himself'. Wherein, therefore, lies the essential conflict of values?

In traditional ideology the individual was dignified by the integrity and sovereignty of his or her own ego, as his or her conduct was compatible with a moral code which had its origins in the decalogue. To put it simply, the new system substituted loyalty to the collective for dignity, where the collective was itself formed with reference to ideological values and conduct compatible with the expectations of the authorities. For the authorities have usurped the right to determine what is good and what is bad for society. As a result of this arbitrary process of definition, the expectations of the authorities with regard to the individual can be identified with those of the community and thus interpreted as the social norm. This is achieved through the control of public language and an instrumental approach to the law. In this kind of system the law sometimes designates human behaviour as incompatible with the generally accepted norms of social co-existence. These are the norms which the centre introduces into the controlled public domain and which it itself designates as accepted. Deviations from these norms are then apt to be regarded as forms of social or even psychological deviance.

The value system of the ruling class allows the autonomy of any individual to be denied. The argument is that this may be necessary during what is called the process of construction of the new system. In this process social relationships are classified according to two basic categories in the class struggle: (a) relationships based on favours to political allies, referred to in the official semantic code as the ruling class, and (b) relationships implying the repression of political foes, referred to variously as class enemies, anti-socialist forces and so on. Under these conditions the self-determination of a person who does not belong among political allies and who as a result does not perform the tasks designated for him or her by the political centre has to be denied for the sake of the 'higher goal', that is the construction of a perfect social system. It is only after the mythical accomplishment of this objective that it is possible to construct real self-determination of the individual on the basis of the coherent value system of the ruling class, since it is only then that all other values from earlier historical epochs will have been supplanted by these new values. In other words, people will only be truly liberated when they are able to perceive reality solely in terms of the official value system.

That is why the freedom of the individual during the 'transitional period' is only relative. The limits of this freedom are set by the construction goals of the new system. A person is free only in so far as his or her individual behaviour is compatible with the general objectives of the reconstruction of the social and political order. These limits to freedom shift as the current political interests of the ruling group change. What was forbidden during the Stalinist period became acceptable after October 1956; what was normal daily practice in public life during the Solidarity period was forbidden activity after the introduction of martial law, and so on.

According to doctrine and the nature of the public life associated with this doctrine, it is not the system which should be adjusted to people and their aspirations, but rather the reverse: it is people, their way of conceiving the world and their individual needs which should be adjusted to the abstract central project in the course of an intensive indoctrination process. This point has been made by Szczepański, who has written:

> The socialist system has not gradually been developing within the capitalist system as capitalism grew up within feudalism. And so while the personality of the economic man of capitalism was also gradually taking shape, socialism has to introduce its own personality type only after victorious revolution. . . . During the early phase of socialist construction an essential role is ascribed to education. That is why the socialist educational ideal has such an important role to play; it defines the basic characteristics of the educated person, of the person who undergoes the educational process, whose attitudes, goals and motives are expected to become the motive power of the socialist economy. (Szczepański 1973: 311–12)

And so an individual experiences two more or less mutually exclusive 'realities' in his or her life. One is the world of public institutions, which function according to the axiology of the ruling class. The other is the world of small social groups or perhaps of religious communities, which function according to the axiology encoded in the national culture.

The Control of Language and Social Dimorphism

Language can be an effective instrument of political control if there is a monopoly of information and propaganda dissemination. In Poland it is power over language, or more precisely, over the semantic code used in public life, which is the most important, but not sufficient, condition for gaining control over minds — or to put it another way, to effectively shape collective consciousness. Instead of a pluralistic exchange of ideas there is a monocentrist semantic code which performs several extremely important political and social functions in the maintainance of the system. Let us mention a few characteristic features of the semantic code which is imposed on the system of communication in the public domain.

(1) The truth does not emerge as a result of debate but is revealed.

(2) The meaning of elements in the semantic code is relative and dependent on their current political usefulness for the centre.

(3) Information and opinions which cannot be accommodated within the official code cannot be broadcast by institutions controlled by the centre but can only be transmitted informally.

(4) Events which cannot be accommodated within the official semantic code do not exist for the centre; this is how the fictitious 'ideological reality' is created.

(5) In the official semantic code there is a built-in symbolism of support for the existing power structure. As long as the centre controls the law and wields sufficient force, this symbolism is a successful substitute for real social support.

(6) Since there is no pluralistic exchange of information and opinions, genuine public opinion is stifled and all attempts to transcend the official code through the public expression of opinion or the dissemination of facts which have no place within the code are regarded as deviant, pathological or downright criminal.

In this way a coherent and stable system is formed. It influences social consciousness while at the same time creating an ideological reality as a substitute for the legitimation of the system. It is theoretically possible for the official semantic code to be handled effectively enough for it to encompass the whole of social consciousness, where ideological reality would be the only reality anyone would perceive. The standard thinking offered by the official code would then become deeply internalised, as would its value system. Fiction would then be transformed into reality in Durkheim's sense of a social fact. Society would be 'educated in the spirit of the ideals' of the doctrines imposed by the centre, and the state of affairs for which the centre is striving would have been attained. In this state of perfection it would no longer be necessary to use violence or the threat of violence. Society would become an amorphous helpless mass of individuals rearranged according to each political purpose of the centre. These individuals would not only obey every order and be incapable of any independent course of action, but because of their helplessness they would also look for orders, cues and suggestions in order for them to retain a sense of

Crisis and Transition

meaningfulness and security. In this kind of model society it is not
so much the centre which depends on the individuals in the controlled community but, *vice versa*, each individual depends on the
centre, and not only in a political sense. What I have in mind here is
a deeper kind of dependence whereby one rids oneself of one's
existential anxieties. This is what happens when obedience to the
centre becomes a person's destiny. Orders are obeyed with zeal, one
affirms oneself, gives heightened meaning to one's existence and
increases one's sense of security. However, the creation and main-
tenance of the ideological reality requires a specific approach to the
fundamental value of truth.

Truth in an Authoritarian Political System

Cicero once wrote: 'I am eager to find the truth and I mean what I
say. How could I not desire to find the truth if I enjoy the discovery
of anything even approaching it. But while I consider the recogni-
tion of the truth to be the most beautiful thing, I consider the ugliest
to be the declaration of falsehood as truth' (1961: 93). Today in the
epoch of the mass media and public opinion, the truth more than
ever has become a political category. The mass media have made
public opinion, in addition to traditional mechanisms of political
democracy, a way of controlling what the politicians do. It is thus
natural that politicians have attempted to mould public opinion in
ways which might give them more leeway, extend their electoral
support or prolong their power.

Where there is a pluralist public life in a polycentric social order
there are independent sources of information and different and
often competing centres for the creation of opinion. Under these
conditions the truth about reality emerges from public debate, from
a clash of opinion and from a verification of the facts through
comparison of information from various sources such as govern-
ments, oppositions, independent social movements, public-opinion
polls or competing press agencies who have to maintain their
credibility if they hope to sell their news bulletins.

Every power apparatus tries to create the image of reality which
most favours its own interests. This is what I have described as
ideological reality, and it is necessary if power is to be sustained.
However, when influential opinion-forming groups and independent sources of information are present in the public domain, the

power apparatus is not the only agency broadcasting the 'truth' about reality, and it cannot create a complete ideological image of it. As in a court of law, the truth emerges from public controversy; society thus obtains an image of reality which is as close to the truth as is humanly possible. The power apparatus does not totally control language and cannot create any exclusive official semantic code. The language of social communication is not appropriated by the power establishment but belongs to public opinion.

In an authoritarian political system the truth is revealed. The centre not only determines what information will be allowed public currency but also interprets its meaning. News and opinion, signed and sealed by the centre, are 'true' by definition; they are not open to doubt within the officially controlled semantic code. Thus both information and the judgements which run through it and which are formulated by the political centre, are 'absolutely true'. In this context ideological reality does not need controversy as an approach to truth. As soon as the truthfulness of a particular piece of news has been declared, any attempt to undermine it becomes a political act aimed not at the news item but at the political decision underlying it and thus indirectly also at the political decision-makers. Since, again by definition, these decision-makers represent the whole of the political system, any questioning of the truth of an item of political news becomes an act against the system.

Uncontrolled news is by definition aimed against the system and inimical to it. It is thus eliminated from public life by preventive censorship. When this does not work, the sources of such news are persecuted by law, which is also under executive control, or simply in the last resort eliminated by violent means. In the ideal situation the system described here would not have any alternative routes for the circulation of news, nor any opinion-forming centres independent of the ruling elite. In practice, of course, it is rarely the case that any situation remains identical with its Weberian ideal type for even a short historical timespan.

In authoritarian countries the function which is served by alternative routes of news circulation has been taken over primarily by symbolic communication at the level of small informal groups. News is transmitted verbally, and opinions on specific events occurring within primary groups such as the family or circles of friends provide an alternative image of the world. However, even in the most authoritarian socio-political systems, at least within the European cultural tradition, there are always some more or less significant alternative institutional routes for the circulation of information. No system, however centralised, is yet able to form the ideal closed pattern where all institutions are equally subordinated to the centre.

One institution which has succeeded in maintaining its independent status in Poland throughout the whole of the postwar period has been the Roman Catholic Church. During periods of crisis in particular, it has circulated values and, to a lesser extent, information. If one adds to this the foreign radio stations broadcasting in Polish, we have to conclude that in postwar Poland the authoritarianism of the imposed system has never been absolute. Indeed, it never could have been more than a half-measure in view of the Polish national culture.

The linguistic monopoly of the ruling group was first broken in 1979. One of the effects of the Pope's first visit to Poland was that it seriously dented what had seemed an invulnerable aspect of the system: the centre's monopoly of public language. For the first time since the late 1940s, people were able to hear in public what previously they had only heard in small social groups. Truth, freedom, human dignity — these were terms which appealed to values which had consistently been pushed outside the range of the official semantic code. The Pope's first visit proved not only that what was thought in private could be expressed in public but also, and perhaps more importantly, that what the majority had been thinking and saying in private was again contributing to a great commonwealth of values which defined the true image of Polish society. These common values were so strongly and uniformly espoused that they quite unexpectedly turned out to be able to provide a sufficiently solid foundation for the mass protest movement which was to be formed one year later. I would like to emphasise here that I do not share the view that the Pope's first visit was the cause of the Solidarity movement. What I do believe, however, is that it acted as an important catalyst which activated these causes. It was these values which allowed the nationwide social institution known as Solidarity to grow up after August 1980. It was this institution which more than anything broke the rule over public language which was established in Poland after the Second World War.

During the short time when Solidarity existed legally, the language of public life again became public property. Truth was no longer revealed in official announcements but emerged from public debates and social communication, confused as these often were. As soon as the Gdańsk agreements were signed, the law ceased to be an instrument of power but gradually assumed its proper role of regulating social relationships. This process was halted by the imposition of martial law. Alternative opinion-forming centres and independent channels for the circulation of information were pushed out of public life. However, this does not mean that they have ceased to function. Martial law meant the return of dimorphism and an even more polarised social life than had existed before Solidarity.

Social Dimorphism from the Standpoint of the Individual

The centre is probably aware of social dimorphism, or of the fact that there is a rift which cuts off a part of social life where it has no grip. Extreme forms of this phenomenon are officially known as 'internal emigration', while in terms of the present analysis it might be referred to as an escape from ideological reality. Obviously, the centre tries to keep dimorphism to a minimum. As I have mentioned, the long-term objective is to make ideological reality the only reality perceived by the individual. This is a natural aim stemming from the logic of the values of the ruling group. In fact, if an individual only recognised ideological reality, he or she would be liberated from axiological doubt and from external coercion, which would then become redundant. In effect, his or her subjective sense of freedom would be expanded. Indeed, if the world and the individual's place in it were what ideological reality claims it is, and if this were accepted, then the world would become simple and intelligible. It would be split into the realm of absolute good (i.e. that which lies within ideological reality) and absolute evil (i.e. that which lies outside it). A person would then be absolutely free to fulfil his or her strictly limited role. Paradoxically, there is no paradox involved in this. The analogy of a religious order presents itself where, although there are strict rules, those belonging to it do not feel constrained; on the contrary, they see the meaning of life in terms of submission and blind obedience. But it is scarcely possible to turn a whole society into a monastery, particularly if the underlying culture is from the outset inimical to such a project.

I am not familiar with any systematic research into the psychology of personality change under such conditions. The only work to which I have had access was concerned with the Far East.

Lifton (1967) carried out a series of open-ended interviews with Europeans and Asians who had undergone brainwashing in China. Some of what he has to say captures the nature of personality change when an individual is coerced into full acceptance of ideological reality.

> Many things happen psychologically to one exposed to milieu control; the most basic is the disruption between self and outside world. . . . He is deprived of the combination of external information and inner reflection which anyone requires to test the realities of his environment and to maintain a measure of identity separate from it. Instead, he is called upon to make an absolute polarization of the real (the prevailing ideology) and the unreal (everything else). (Lifton 1967: 479)

This is easiest to attain in laboratory conditions or in a closed social setting where the individual is isolated from the disturbing influences of the outside world.

In contemporary Europe perhaps only Albania is sufficiently isolated for successful mind reform on a macro-social scale. However, because of the country's isolation it is difficult for an observer to know anything with more than hypothetical certainty, or rather uncertainty.

The other new thing which the system did to individuals was to require them to prove their 'ideological innocence'. There could be no doubt about the result when one considers the extent to which individuals in their metaphorical or literal isolation can oppose the powerful machinery of repression. In fact, what it was all about was not the quest for truth, but the playing out of a particular kind of psychodrama. The stake in this game was a change in the individual's personality, involving the irrevocable acceptance of ideological reality. As Lifton has remarked, 'closely related to the demand of absolute purity is an obsession with personal confession. Confession is carried beyond its ordinary religious, legal, and therapeutic expressions to the point of becoming a cult in itself. . . . Private ownership of the mind and its products — of imagination and of memory — becomes highly immoral' (1976: 484). The once sharp distinction between the victim and the persecutor becomes blurred. As the change in the victim's personality shifts towards ideological reality, the persecutor gradually becomes educator and guide to the victims on their difficult path to the understanding of their 'errors', the condemnation of these errors and total identification with the persecutor and his value system. When this stage is reached, the process of re-education is complete and, in the terms of the present chapter, this means the elimination of the dimorphism experienced by the individual before personality change. The 'old' value system is completely rejected and displaced by the new one, which is embodied by ideological reality. This is now perceived as the only reality, since the individual is no longer able to understand or accept the world from any other perspective.

Brainwashing techniques have been applied on a laboratory scale only; attempts at mass implementation have not been successful, notwithstanding the intensive efforts which have been made by the centre. An entire society provides too complex an entity for such a project to be feasible. To be successful, two basic conditions would have to be fulfilled: (a) a break in historical continuity and (b) a break in cultural continuity. These conditions were not even met in the extreme situation of Cambodia under the rule of the Khmer Rouge. Distortions of history, to fit in with the current political purposes of the centre, are merely feeble and unsuccessful attempts to meet these two conditions. At best, they can only help to retain a measure of internal coherence in ideological reality. However, they fail in the most important area of reducing social dimorphism and thus extending ideological reality to small social groups and the individuals which form them.

If small social groups cannot be isolated from each other by fear or mistrust, monopoly of information is not total and language control is not complete. Ideological reality is thus undermined. If it is to be effective, people must be unaware of any alternative. That is why the centre must strive to create social isolation and to break down communication on levels other than that of ideological reality. From the point of view of the interests of the political centre, individuals should be able to communicate with each other only within ideological reality and only by means of the official semantic code, thus bringing their thinking into line with the centre's expectations. The cognitive capacity of human beings would be reduced to those concepts which have a place in the official semantic code. We are led by these considerations to the conclusion that social dimorphism is a permanent feature of the social system described here; there is reason to believe that individuals also believe this situation to be relatively permanent.

There is no doubt that the experience of social dimorphism is not a comfortable one. Reality is schizoid, split into two worlds which

173

have little impact on, or contact with, each other. Underlying this state of affairs are two sets of incompatible values. Ideological reality is aggressive in that it attempts to displace the prevalent way of thinking of small groups which is compatible with an earlier cultural heritage, and to replace it with an ideology of its own. On the other hand, individuals who belong to small groups and observe their standards, consciously or unconsciously defend themselves against the expansion of ideological reality. This defence primarily consists of the transmission of traditional values from one generation to the next and in the preservation of great national myths such as the legendary uprising which cannot be fully accommodated within ideological reality. Finally, and perhaps most importantly, under Polish conditions the informal transmission of ideas, values and myths from one generation to the next is underpinned by the powerful Roman Catholic tradition. In this respect religion plays a vital integrating role, and the strong link between religion and the national culture reinforces the world of values which is in collision with ideological reality and with the feeling of community at all levels above that of the small group, from the strictly local to the universal and transnational.

If it is true that individuals experience dimorphism with more or less acute discomfort, then one might expect that there would be a tendency to reduce this discomfort. Theoretically, we may assume three types of dimorphism reduction technique on an individual or group level:

(1) The abandoning of traditional values and the exclusive acceptance of ideological reality.
(2) Withdrawal from public life as far as is possible under a statist system which politicises practically all of public life.
(3) Attempts to change the existing system.

The first approach is adopted by individuals who tend to be recruited to the ruling group. The second approach is typical of individuals who have been referred to as 'inner emigrants'. Finally, the third approach is typical of so-called 'dissidents'. However, these are ideal attitudes in the Weberian sense. In practice people usually opt for a fourth approach, that is a continuous series of compromises between the requirements of the ideological reality to which public life is subject and the requirements of the acknowledged system of values obtaining outside public life. This attitude seems to be associated with the belief that dimorphism is a permanent feature of the system in which people must live and that this fact has to be accepted.

Can the existence of social dimorphism be regarded as a significant factor in social change? It certainly does not play a direct role in this regard, but it does provide a social context which favours change. This is corroborated by the phenomenon which may be metaphorically referred to as social super-conductivity and which occurred in the early days of Solidarity. The social situation was by then ripe for change, and any pretext could serve as the trigger. The vitality of the world of social groups, the private world with its specific values, turned out to form the anchor for the protests, so that what was a conflict of interests rapidly became a conflict of values.

As we know, a conflict of interests need not become total conflict threatening the basis of the social order if the opponents have values in common. However, a conflict of values necessarily involves issues of the most fundamental nature which are essential for the survival of the system. Such a conflict cannot be resolved within the system, but requires that it totally or partially change.

Some Methodological Remarks

The theoretical position outlined above has certain significant methodological implications. If we assume that social dimorphism exists, then a number of questions arise concerning the nature of empirical sociology. In particular, doubts arise as to what in fact empirical social research is studying, particularly when it is concerned with social consciousness. Will such research only reflect elements of ideological reality, or will it be able to transcend it? It is not easy to give a categorical answer to this question. It is true that sociology occupies a specific institutional place in that public life which is controlled by the centre. Sociology and the research which is carried out under its aegis can thus be regarded by those taking part in the research as belonging to the world of institutions; they are thus likely to be on the defensive as they always are when they face the alien institutional world. Above all, respondents are apt to revert to the official semantic code as the channel of communication between themselves and the sociologist. In such cases it is inevitable that research revolves within the closed sphere of ideological reality and thus unwittingly reflects only one of the two sides of social life. In practice, things are even more complicated. The defensive reactions of respondents may be supposed to depend on the following circumstances:

(1) The degree of trust the respondents feel towards the institution represented by the researcher.
(2) The nature of the research problem, or to be more precise, the extent to which it is accommodated within the official semantic code.
(3) The degree of repressiveness exhibited by the institutional world towards individuals when their actions and attitudes are incompatible with institutional expectations.

It may be assumed that the less respondents trust a given institution, the more easily the research problem is accommodated within the official semantic code; and the greater the degree of institutional repression, the more likely it is that empirical data will apply solely to ideological reality. It will thus have scant value in the prediction of social change such as crisis, rebellion or revolution. On the other hand, the greater the confidence in a given institution, the more the research problem transcends the official semantic code; and the more tolerant the institutional world, the more probable it is that an insight may be gained into that side of social life which lies beyond the boundaries of what is public. It is clear that in Poland, and probably elsewhere also, how far the conditions above are met depends on how successful sociology is in gaining institutional independence from the political control centre, and on how far it is allowed to transcend the official semantic code. Polish empirical sociology is thus confronted with two fairly dramatic alternatives: either it will be independent or it will lose all significance. Time will tell which will be the case.

Bibliography

Adamski, W., I. Białecki, K. Jasiewicz, L. Kolarska, A. Mokrzyszewski, A. Rychard, and J. Sikorska (1981), *Polacy '80* (The Poles 1980), Warsaw

Adamski, W., L. Beskid, E. Iliasiewicz, K. Jasiewicz, L. Kolarska, A. Mokrzyszewski, A. Rychard, J. Sikorska, A. Titków, and E. Wnuk-Lipiński (1982), *Polacy '81* (The Poles 1981), Warsaw

Adamski, W., K. Jasiewicz, A. Rychard (eds) (1986), *Raport z badania Polacy '84. Dynamika konfliktu i konsensusu* (Report on the research: Poles '84. Dynamics of conflict and consensus), Warsaw

Bednarski, M. (1984), 'Drugi obieg' (The second lap), *Życie Gospodarcze*, no. 35, 8 August

Bialer, S. (1983), 'The question of legitimacy', in D. Held et al. (eds), *States and Societies*, New York

Brunner, G. (1982), 'Legitimacy doctrines and legitimation procedures in East European systems', in Rigby and Feher (eds) (1982)

Buber, M. (1983), 'Między społeczeństwem a państwem' (Betwixt society and state), *Więź*, nos. 11–12

Cicero, M.T. (1961), *Pisma Filozoficzne* (Philosophical writings), vol. 3, Warsaw

Czołoszyński, T. (n.d.), 'Tendencje zróżnicowania dochodów w latach 70-tych' (Trends in income differentials in the 1970s), unpublished typescript

Etzioni, A. (1961), *A Comparative Analysis of Complex Organisations*, New York

Feher, F. (1982), 'Paternalism as a Mode of Legitimation in East European Societies', in Rigby and Feher (eds) (1982)

Furbotn, J., and S. Pejovich (n.d.), 'Property rights and economic theory', *Journal of Economic Literature*, vol. 10

Góralska, A. (1981), 'Analiza rozpiętości dochodów' (An analysis of highest and lowest incomes), paper read at a meeting of the Polish Economics Society, 28 April

Gross, J. (1982), 'Totalitarianism', *Soviet Studies*, no. 3

Gulczyński, M. (1982), *Bariera aspiracji* (The aspirations barrier), Warsaw

Habermas, J. (1976), *Legitimation Crisis*, London

—— (1979), *Communication and the Evolution of Society*, Boston

Bibliography

Heller, A. (1982), 'Phases of legitimation in Soviet-type societies', in Rigby and Feher (eds) (1982)

Hirszowicz, M., and W. Morawski (1967), *Z badań nad społecznym uczestnictwem w organizacji przemysłowej* (Studies in participation in industrial organisations), Warsaw

Janicka, K. (1987), 'Różnice społeczne w potocznym odczuciu' (Perception of social differences), in Koralewicz (ed.) (1987)

Jarosz, M. (1981), 'Samobójstwo — wskaźnik społecznej dezintegracji' (Suicide as an index of social disintegration), paper read at the Sixth Polish Sociological Congress, Warsaw

Jasińska, A. (1984), 'Rationalisation and legitimation crisis: the relevance of Marxian and Weberian works for an explanation of the political order's legitimacy crisis in Poland', unpublished typescript

——, and R. Siemieńska (1981), 'O racjonalności postaw przedstawicieli władzy terenowej w przededniu kryzysu' (The rationality of attitudes among local authority representatives on the eve of the crisis), paper presented at the 'Crisis and Conflict' conference in Radziejówice in May

Jaśkiewicz, L. (1979), *Carat i ziemstwa na przełomie XIX i XX w.* (The Czarist system and land self-government at the turn of the nineteenth century), Warsaw

Jedlicki, W. (1961), *Co sądzić o freudyzmie i psychoanalizie?* (What are we to think of Freudianism and psychoanalysis?), Warsaw

Jermakowicz, W. (1981), 'Rzeczpospolita samorządna' (The self-governing republic), *Przegląd Techniczny*, no. 40

Kamiński, A. (1983), 'Niedialektyczna koncepcja planowania i interes społeczny' (Non-dialectic planning concepts and the social interest), in W. Morawski (ed.), *Demokracja i gospodarka*

—— (1984), *Monopol i konkurencja* (Monopoly and competition), Warsaw

Kaniowski, A. (1976), 'Habermasowska koncepcja kapitalizmu' (Habermas's concept of capitalism), *Studia Filozoficzne*, no. 8

Kępiński, A. (1977), *Lęk* (Anxiety), Warsaw

Kiciński, K. (1987), 'Sytuacja zagrożenia a sądy moralne' (Threatening situations and moral judgements), in Koralewicz (ed.) (1987)

Klakson (1982), 'Łowcza', in *Szpilki*

Koralewicz-Zębik, J. (1979), 'Niektóre przemiany systemu wartości, celów i orientacji życiowych społeczeństwa polskiego' (Changes in value systems, goals and life orientation in Polish society), *Studia Socjologiczne*, no. 4

—— (1983a), *Lęk a postrzeganie ładu społecznego* (Anxiety and the perception of the social order), Polish Academy of Sciences Institute of Philosophy and Sociology, Warsaw

—— (1983b), 'Postawy wobec zewnętrznego przymusu: podłoże psychospołeczne sierphia 80' (Attitudes towards coercion: the psycho-social background to August 1980), in A. Siciński (ed.), *Style zycia, obyczaje,*

ethos w Polsce lat siedemdziesiątych z perspektywy roku 1981, Warsaw
—— (1984), 'The perception of inequality in Poland 1956–80', *Sociology*, vol. 18, no. 2

Koralewicz, J. (formerly Koralewicz-Zębik) (ed.) (1987), *Społeczeństwo polskie przed kryzysem w świetle badań socjologicznych 1977–79* (Polish society before the crisis in the light of sociological research 1977–1979), Warsaw

Kostecki, M. (1981), 'Polskie lato i inne pory roku' (The Polish summer and other seasons), *Problemy Ekonomiczne*, March

Krasucki, P., K. Nowak and J. Mierzwińska (1984), 'Problemy życia codziennego i warunków zdrowotnych różnych grup pracowników: wstępny raport z badań' (Problems of everyday life and health conditions in different occupational groups: a preliminary research report), unpublished typescript

Kruczkowska, G. (1979), *Egalitaryzm a płace* (Egalitarianism and income), Warsaw

Krzak, M. (1983), 'Budżet 1982' (The 1982 budget), *Życie Gospodarcze*, no. 15

Kuczyński, P. (1984), 'Robotnicy i nowomowa' (Manual workers and newspeak), unpublished typescript

Kurczewski, J. (1981), *Konflikt i solidarność* (Conflict and Solidarity), Wydawnictwo Związkowe

Kurowicki, J. (1983), *Biurokratyzm i władza* (Bureaucracy and power), Warsaw

Lamentowicz, W. (1982), 'Legitymizacja władzy politycznej w powojennej Polsce' (The legitimation of political power in post-war Poland), unpublished typescript

Lane, D. (1976), *The Socialist Industrial Estate*, London

Łazarski, A. (1982), 'Świadomość partyina' (Party consciousness), unpublished typescript

Lifton, R.J. (1976), *Thought Reform and the Psychology of Totalism: A Study of 'Brainwashing' in China*, London

Lindberg, L.N., et al. (eds) (1975), *Stress and Contradiction in Modern Capitalism*, Lexington, Mass.

Lindenberg, G. (1986), *Zmiana społeczna a świadomość polityczna. Dynamika postaw politycznych studentów Warszawy 1979–83* (Social changes and political consciousness. Dynamics of political attitudes of Warsaw students 1979–83), Warsaw

Lipset, S.M. (1959), *Political Man*, London

Malec, J. (1980), *Poglądy społeczeństwa polskiego na przestepczość* (Polish attitudes to crime), Warsaw

Malewski, A. (1975), 'Rozdwięk między uznawanyni przekonanianami i jego konsekwencje' (Inconsistencies in declared convictions and their consequences), in *O nowy kształt nauk społecznych*, Warsaw

179

Mann, M. (1975), 'The ideology of intellectuals and other people in the development of capitalism', in Lindberg et al. (eds) (1975)

Markus, M. (1981), 'Crisis of legitimation and workers' movement: Understanding Poland', *Thesis Eleven*, no. 3

—— (1982), 'Overt and covert modes of legitimation in East European societies', in Rigby and Feher (eds) (1982)

Marody M. (1986), '"Collective sense" and stability or change of the social order', paper presented at the Polish–British conference on legitimacy, Nieboròw/Warsaw, June 1986

—— (1987), *Technologia intelektu* (The technology of intellect), Warsaw

——, J. Kolbowski, C. Łabanowska, K. Nowak, and A. Tyszkiewicz (1981), *Polacy '80* (The Poles 1980), University of Warsaw Institute of Sociology, mimeo

Marody, M., and K. Nowak (1983), 'Wartości a działania' (Values and action), *Studia Socjologiczne*, no. 4, pp. 5–29

Marx, K. (1966), 'Precapitalist economic formations — a fragment', *Studia Ekonomiczne*, no. 15

Mayntz, R. (1975), 'Legitimacy and the directive capacity of the political system', in Lindberg et al. (eds) (1975)

Michałczyk, T. (1983), 'Młodzież robotnicza a sobie' (Young manual workers talking about themselves), in B. Gołębiowski and E. Śmiłowski (eds), *Młoda generacja polaków w okresie kryzysu*, Opole

Milic-Czerniak, R. (1985), 'Doba często zbyt krótka' (The day is often too short), *Życie Gospodarcze*, 6 January

Morawski, W. (1973), *Samorząd robotniczy w gospodarce socjalistycznej* (Worker self-management in a socialist economy), Warsaw

—— (1980), 'Społeczeństwo a narzucona industrializacja' (Society and imposed industrialisation), *Kultura*, 7 December

Narojek, W. (1984), 'Perspektywy pluralizmu w upaństwowionym społeczenstwie' (The future of pluralism in a statist society), unpublished typescript

Newcomb, T.M. (1956), 'Two types of orientation toward obstacles', in idem (ed.), *Social psychology*, New York

North, D.C., and R.P. Thomas (1973), *The Rise of the Western World*, Cambridge

Nowak, K. (1984), 'Kryzys legitymizacji władzy w Polsce z perspektywy zycia codziennego' (The crisis in power legitimation in Poland from the perspective of everyday life), in S. Nowak (ed.), *Społeczeństwo polskie czasu kryzysu*, University of Warsaw Institute of Sociology, mimeo, Warsaw

Nowak, S. (1965), *Przemiany społecznej struktury w świadomości społecznej* (Changes in social structure in social consciousness), Warsaw

—— (1979), *System Wartości Społeczeństwa Polskiego* (Polish society's value system), *Studia Socjologizne*, no. 4

—— and G. Lindenberg (1984), 'Studenci Warszawy' (Warsaw's students), unpublished typescript

Offe, C. (1975), 'Introduction to Part II' in Lindberg et al. (eds) (1975)

—— (1976), *Industry and Equality*, Birkenhead

Ossowski, S. (1967a), *Dzieła* (The collected works), vol. III, Warsaw

—— (1967b), *Dzieła* (The collected works), vol. IV, Warsaw

—— (1968), *Dzieła* (The collected works), vol. V, Warsaw

Otawska, E. (1976), *Nasze miejsce w społeczeństwie* (Our place in society), Centre for the Study of Public Opinion, mimeo, Warsaw

Pacewicz, P. (1983), *Pomiędzy myslą a rzeczywistością: rewolucia społeczna jako zjawisko psychologiczne* (Between thought and reality: social revolution as a psychological phenomenon), Wrocław

Pakulski, J. (1986), 'Legitimacy and Mass Compliance: Reflections on Max Weber and Soviet-Type Societies', *British Journal of Political Science*, vol. 16

Pańków, W. (1981a), 'Polskie lato 1980. Kryzys systemu władzy' (The Polish summer of 1980: the crisis of the power system), unpublished typescript

—— (1981b), 'Reform gospodarcza a uspołecznienie własnosci' (Economic reform and the socialisation of ownership), *Kultura*, 15 February

—— (1982a), 'The "Polish summer": A crisis of the system of power', *Sisyphus*, vol. 3

—— (1982b), 'Partia państwo gospodarka' (The party, state and economy), unpublished typescript

—— (1983), 'Stan wojenny w Polsce: ciagłość czy zmiana systemu władzy?' (Martial law in Poland: continuity or change in the power system?), unpublished typescript

Piotrowska-Hochfeld (1982), 'Decyduje załoga' (The workforce decides), *Polityka*, no. 1314, 10 July

Podgórecki, A. (1966), *Prestiž prawa* (The prestige of the law), Warsaw

Reykowski, J. (1978), 'Podstawowe mechanizmy regulacji społecznego zachowania się człowieka' (Basic mechanisms for the regulation of pro-social behaviour in man), in J. Reykowski (ed.), *Teoria osobowości a zachowanie prospołeczne*, Warsaw

—— (1979), *Motywacje, postawy prospołeczne, osobowość* (Motivation, pro-social attitudes, personality), Warsaw

—— (1985), 'O alienacji politycznej w polsce' (Political alienation in Poland), *Polityka* no. 14, 6 April

Rigby, T.H. and F. Feher (eds) (1982), *Political Legitimation in Communist States*, New York

Rychard, A. (1980), *Reforma gospodarcza: socjologiczna analiza związków polityki i gospodarki* (Economic reform: a sociological analysis of the links between politics and economics), Wrocław

—— (1981), 'Organizacja w systemie zarządzania a potrzeby społeczne'

(Organisation in the management system and social needs), *Organizacja i Kierowanie*, no. 1

—— (1983), 'Makt, ekonomii, intressem: tve paradigm for anallys av samhallsskicket', in H. Wiberg et al. (eds), *Konkflikt och Solidaritet i Polen*, Stockholm

—— (1984), 'Władza i interesy w gospodarce' (Power and interests in the economy), unpublished typescript

Seligman, M. (1975), *Helplessness: On Depression, Development and Death*, San Francisco

Sikorska, J. (1983), 'Społeczna mapa potrzeb i aspiraji konsumpcynych' (The social map of consumer needs and aspirations), unpublished typescript

——, A. Rychard and W. Wnuk-Lipiński (forthcoming), 'Nie-równości społeczne w Polsce' (Social inequalities in Poland), in E. Wnuk-Lipiński (ed.), *Nierówności w Polsce*, Warsaw

Skalski, E. (1981), 'Porozumienia czy fasada?' (Agreement or façade?), *Tygodnik Solidarnosci*, no. 36

Skir, J. (n.d.), 'Reform gospodarcza po roku, kilka refleksji' (The economic reform one year on: some reflections), *Krytyka*, no. 15

Smith, K.H., and B. Richards (1967), 'Effects of a rational appeal and of anxiety on conformity behaviour', *Journal of Personality and Social Psychology*, vol. 5, no. 1

Staniszkis, J. (1979), 'Typologia technik kierowania w organizacji' (A typology of management techniques in organisations), in W. Morawski (ed.), *Kierowanie w społeczeństwie*, Warsaw

—— (1981), 'Rewolucji nie robi się, ona przychodzi sama' (Revolution is not made, it comes by itself), *Wektory*, no. 1

—— (1986), 'Stability without legitimation. An attempt at interpretation', paper presented at the conference of the Polish Sociological Association on legitimacy, Warsaw, April 1986

Stein, M.R., et al. (eds) (1965), *Identity and Anxiety*, New York

Strzelecki, J. (1983), 'Polski kryzys gospodarczy jako koniec industriali-zacji socjalistycznej' (The Polish economic crisis as the end of socialist industrialisation), paper read at a seminar at the Polish Academy of Sciences Institute of Philosophy and Sociology, Warsaw

—— (1984), 'Polskie neurozy' (The Polish neuroses), paper read at A. Siciński's seminar at the Polish Academy of Sciences, Warsaw

—— (forthcoming), *Socjalizmu model liryczny* (Socialism: a lyrical model)

Sułek, A. (1984), 'Przemiany wartości życiowych młodziezy polskiej: winiki badań — obserwacje — spekulacje' (Changes in life values among Polish young people: empirical findings — observations — speculation), in S. Nowak (ed.), *Społeczeństwo polskie czasu kryzysu*, University of Warsaw Institute of Sociology, mimeo, Warsaw

Surdykowski, J. (n.d.), 'Zreformować reformę' (Reforming the reform),

Życie Literackie, no. 1532

Świda, H. (1987), 'Młodzież licealna schyłku lat 70ych' (Secondary school pupils in the late 1970s), in Koralewicz (ed.) (1987)

Szawiel, T. (1982), 'Struktura społeczna i postawy a grupy ethosowe: O możliwości ewolucji społecznej' (Social structure and attitudes and ethos groups: the possibility of social evolution), *Studia Sociologiczne*, nos. 1/2

Szczepański, J. (1973), *Odmiany czasu teraźniejszego* (Variations of the present), Warsaw

Sztompka, P. (1983), 'Zmiana Strukturalna Społeczeństwa: Szkic Teorii' (Structural change in society: a tentative theory), *Studia Socjologiczne*

Szwarc, K. (1981), 'Samorząd załogi a reforma gospodarcza' (Worker self-management and economic reform), in *Samorząd załogi — model a rzeczywistość*, Warsaw

Tarkowski, J. (1986), 'Economic efficiency as a substitute for legitimacy in postwar Poland', paper presented at the Polish–British conference on legitimacy, Nieborów/Warsaw, June 1986

Touraine A. (1984a), 'Socjologia akcjonalistyczna' (Action sociology), in E. Mokrzycki (ed.), *Kryzys i schizma*, vol. II, Warsaw

—— (1984b), 'Racje i cele socjologii działania' (The *raison d'être* of a sociology of action), in E. Mokrzycki (ed.), *Kryzys i Schizma*, vol. II

——, F. Dubet, M. Weviorka, and J. Strzelecki (1983), *Solidarity: Poland 1980–81*, Cambridge

Turner, R. (1962), 'Role taking: process versus conformity', in A. Rose (ed.), *Behaviour and Social Process*, Boston

Vaughan, G.M., and K.D. White, (1966), 'Conformity and authoritarianism re-examined'. *Journal of Personality and Social Psychology*, vol. 3, no. 3

Weber, M. (1922), *Wirtschaft und Gesellschaft*, Tubingen

—— (1972), 'Typy władzy prawomocnej' (Types of legitimate power), in J. Kurnal (ed.), *Twórcy naukowych podstaw organizacji*, Warsaw

—— (1975), 'Trzy typy prawomocnego panowania' (Three types of legitimate rule), in J. Szacki (ed.), *Elementy Teorii Sojologicznych*, Warsaw

—— (1976), 'Social causes of the decline of ancient civilisation', in *Economic Theory and Ancient Society*, London

Wesołowski, W. (1974), *Klasy, warstwy i władza* (Classes, strata and power), Warsaw; London, 1979.

——, and B. Mach (1983), 'Systemowe funkcje ruchliwości społecznej', *Kultura i Społeczeństwo*, no. 4; translated as 'Unfulfilled systemic functions of Social Mobility', Parts I and II, *International Sociology* (1986), nos. 1–2

Wiatr, J.J. (1982), 'Problematyka zaspokojania potrzeb ludności a funkcjonowanie polskiego systemu politycznego' (The satisfaction of the population's needs and the Polish political system), in W. Wesołowski (ed.), *Nauki polityczne a potrzeby praktyki*, Warsaw

Wierzbicki, Z.R. (1983), 'Bank czy nadal kasa?' (The bank or still the teller's booth?), *Życie Gospodarcze*, no. 13

Wnuk-Lipiński, E. (1982), 'Dimorphism of values and social schizophrenia: a tentative description', *Sisyphus*, vol. 3, Warsaw

—— (1987), 'Nierownośći i Niesprawiedliwości w Społecznej Świadomości' (Inequalities and injustices in social consciousness), report, Polish Academy of Sciences Institute of Philosophy and Sociology, Warsaw